Balanchine

Russian-American Ballet Master Emeritus

By Reine Duell Bethany

Branden Books, Boston

Library of Congress Cataloging-in-Publication Data

Bethany, Reine.
  Balanchine : Russian-American ballet master emeritus / By Reine
Bethany. -- First edition
      pages cm
  Includes bibliographical references and index.
  ISBN 978-0-8283-2457-1 (pbk. : alk. paper) -- ISBN (invalid)
978-0-8283-2458-8 (ebook)
  1. Balanchine, George. 2. Choreographers--United States--
Biography. I. Title.

  GV1785.B32B48 2012
  792.8'2092--dc23

  [B]

                                    2012030439

ISBN 9780828324571 Paperback Edition
ISBN 9780828324588 E-Book Edition

[BALANCHINE is a Trademark of The George Balanchine Trust.
Direct quotes of George Balanchine are used with permission from
The George Balanchine Trust.]

Branden Books PO Box 812094 Wellesley MA 02482
www.brandenbooks.com

Table of Contents

Introduction

They can all be seen in one theater, on the same breathtaking night:

A man in Shakespearean cape and tunic leaps high into the air, traveling backward at tremendous speed, and vanishes into the wings.

Seventeen women wearing long fluffy skirts float through dreamlike bends and twirls.

Eight men in starkly designed T-shirts and tights define sharp, powerful shapes and patterns, led by two equally striking couples, to piano music that sounds like an unleashed tiger.

A cowboy darts and bounds through a line of dance-hall girls who are frolicking on their tiptoes.

These images are from ballets created by George Balanchine, America's great 20th-century ballet master. His choreography is renowned for its beauty and originality. It demands unusual speed, lightness, and expressiveness from his dancers.

Yet George Balanchine called himself a potato.

Each type of potato, he said, needs just the right soil.

Calling himself a potato exemplified Balanchine's sense of humor. He himself was a dancer—slender, powerful, flexible, expressive—not much like a lumpy root vegetable. Yet his metaphor was apt: In the soil best suited to it, a potato not only grows large and healthy, it sprouts other potatoes.

Balanchine's search for the right soil began when he was a young dancer during the Russian Revolution. He was trained in the best of Russian ballet schools, but by the time he was 16 years old, he was obviously a different sort of potato.

With the adventurousness of youth and the confidence of budding genius, at age 20 George Balanchine left his native soil. He began a risky, at times heartbreaking search for the soil in which he as a dancer and choreographer could thrive. His search took him across three continents and through at least eight nations. It encompassed forms of ballet ranging from the experimental to the ultra-traditional, from opera to vaudeville, from Broadway to film, and even to the Ringling Brothers Circus. Yet nowhere did Balanchine find what he was looking for.

Then he did what great artists do: he created soil of his own. From the soil created by this Russian-born man sprouted a spectacularly American dance troupe, the New York City Ballet. From the New York City Ballet sprouted ballet companies across America. More than a quarter-century after Balanchine's death, these companies are still going strong. Meanwhile, Balanchine ballets are performed by dance troupes on all six inhabited continents.

George Balanchine generated an amazing new crop of potatoes. His accomplishments seem especially remarkable when we think about him at the age of nine. That is when he was first put into ballet school.

He promptly ran away.

Chapter 1
The Sprout Finds Out What He's About (1904—1914)

When young Georgi fled the Imperial School of Theatre and Ballet, he was a slim little boy alone on the streets of St. Petersburg, the capital city of the Russian empire. Why did no one stop him to ask if he was lost?

The likely answer is that he did not look lost. His action was targeted. He proceeded straight to his Aunt Nadia's apartment, from which he and his family had moved only four years before.

Georgi Balanchivadze was born in St. Petersburg on January 22, 1904. His father's name was Meliton, so Georgi's middle name was Melitonovich, son of Meliton. His mother's name was Maria Nikolayevna. Brilliant music shaped Georgi's early life, for Meliton and Maria were highly trained musicians. Meliton was originally from a nation 1,800 miles south of St. Petersburg called Georgia, which Russia had conquered and forced to be part of the Russian empire. Georgi considered himself as much Georgian as Russian.

Born two years on either side of Georgi were his older sister Tamara and his younger brother Andrei. The three tiny Balanchivadze children had no idea their nation was slowly exploding from within. Ruled by a tsar, or emperor, Russian society was officially divided into classes such as Nobility, Merchant, and Peasant. Many Russian citizens believed that this class-based society unfairly favored the Nobility. They furiously claimed that Merchants and Peasants were denied fair land ownership, education, and jobs.

Violent opposition to Tsar Nicholas II and his wife Alexandra brewed in taverns and universities. Russia tilted wildly toward the revolution of the century. But inside the Balanchivadze home, Meliton and Maria played entrancing music on their piano. They gathered friends and family to sing folk songs and opera pieces that

Meliton had collected from the mountains of Georgia. At one point Maria won so much money in a lottery that her delighted husband moved his family into a roomy apartment on a shady street. Aunt Nadia came to live with them. Later, Meliton moved his family to a country home near Lounatiokki (a village in what is now Finland), while Aunt Nadia stayed in the apartment.

One day on the piano bench in the Lounatiokki home, Georgi's destiny began. He was wiggling through yet another beginner piece assigned to him by the piano teacher his mother had hired. He wanted to be outside, running with his pet pig and digging vegetables from the family garden. If he got through his pieces, he could be in motion soon . . . but then something unexpected happened. He was playing a simple Beethoven sonata. Suddenly its chords and melody assembled into a sound that reached his very soul. Splendor and loveliness seemed to speak to him from heaven—a deep, essential joy. After that, he practiced his assigned pieces with intense fascination. He and Andrei became skillful at piano duets.

Georgi's dreams of manhood did not center on music, though. He envisioned a fine military officer's uniform. Or maybe he would be a Russian Orthodox priest like his uncle in St. Petersburg at the Cathedral of Our Lady of Kazan. As a priest, Georgi would chant the strong prayers of the Orthodox service, while a boys' choir would send thrilling melodies upward to the colorful stained-glass windows.

Unfortunately, Meliton was a better musician than a money manager. He bought a share in a restaurant, but gave too many free meals to his friends to make a profit. Finally the government made him straighten out his debts.

All that beautiful extra money was gone.

Again the Balanchivadze family had to live on Meliton's modest musician's income. How could Tamara, Georgi, and Andrei be educated for high-earning careers? The only way was for them to be accepted into schools that were supported by Tsar Nicholas II from tax money. Once accepted, they would live at the schools until they grew up and were employed by the tsarist government.

When Tamara was 11 and Georgi was 9, Maria took them on the slow train ride from Lounatiokki to St. Petersburg. There the children would apply to government schools. The threesome stopped first at the naval academy to enroll Georgi, but to his disappointment, the academy was full; he would have to reapply next year.

Then Maria, with Georgi in tow, took Tamara to try out at the Imperial School of Theatre and Ballet on Theatre Street. Tamara's fantasies centered on the world-famous Russian company known as the Maryinsky Ballet. She had failed the Imperial School audition the year before. While she changed anxiously into dance clothes, Maria and Georgi sat on a bench. A friend of Maria's at the school passed by and suggested that Georgi audition, too. If he got in, his education and career would be taken care of.

Ballet? Audition for the ballet school? Though male ballet dancers were honored in Russian society, becoming one had never entered Georgi's head. He liked playing piano with Andrei when family gathered at the Lounatiokki house. He confidently delivered his lines onstage when his parents put him in community plays. But doing dances in front of everyone— that he couldn't stand.

So it was only through obedience to his mother that he walked across the vast wooden floor of the dance studio. The judges who eyed his movements were top-tier Maryinsky Ballet dancers such as Olga Preobrajenska. A health official made sure he had a straight spine and healthy teeth. He returned to his waiting mother with relief when all *that* was over.

But he was in for a shock: the ballet school accepted him. Returning to Lounatiokki with his mother was not an option: he must start boarding at the Imperial School that very day!

His whole life until that moment disappeared with his mother's retreating back as she left the school. Tamara, too, had been accepted (though she was soon dismissed because she could not keep up; she later became a visual artist). But she and Georgi were assigned to separate boys' and girls' dormitories, so she could provide no comfort to him.

The rest of that day was an orderly nightmare. Supper was not one of the meals Georgi enjoyed cooking with his mother, using

Georgian herbs and spices. No, it was a simple vegetable-meat stew, eaten in an austere dining room where he knew no one but Tamara. Instead of falling asleep under his own blankets while his parents softly played piano in the living room, Georgi mounted steep stairs to a long, high-windowed hall. There he and 28 other boys slept in small beds arranged in long rows.

That night, or perhaps a few days later, Georgi enacted his own nine-year-old-boy solution to this mess. He watched for an opportunity, walked out of the school, and marched to Aunt Nadia's. Surely she would see how unreasonable it was for an aspiring naval officer to be enrolled as a dance student!

Aunt Nadia saw no such thing. She saw a free education and a lifelong job being thrown away by her young relative. The very next morning, she stood with Georgi before the school officials, pleading his return. In their stern yet kind way, they took him back.

Only in later years did the man George Balanchine comment on the desperate loneliness he felt during his first year at the Imperial School. The boy Georgi kept his feelings hidden. Maybe he disliked putting his own clothes away until weekends and wearing a uniform of lightweight pants and shirt for his classes, but he did not say so. Sometimes tears formed deep inside when other students went home on weekends, leaving him without companions because his family could only come get him now and then. But he kept the tears hidden.

The pattern for his life was set by age nine: he did not *react* to bad circumstances. No, he *acted* on them. When he was lonely, he found things to do. Pianos were used in the dance studios to provide musical accompaniment for exercises and rehearsals. On Saturdays the school authorities let Georgi play as much as he wished. The Georgian folksongs his father had taught him rolled from his fingers, as well as classical pieces. He could experience again the heavenly feeling that came to him on the piano bench of the Lounatiokki home and be comforted. On Sundays, he would stand in the Orthodox Russian chapel in the theater building, enthralled with the rainbow colors of the mosaic tiles and the sunlight through the stained-glass windows.

He also tended to be a loner in his dance and academic classes. Georgi was not one to make friends readily. His mind was too focused for him to find fun in random horseplay. Also, the boys teased him. His upper lip sometimes twitched upward unawares, exposing his front teeth, so the other little boys called him "Rat."

Georgi just shrugged when teased. Soon the other boys left him alone, except for one who taunted Georgi constantly, determined to force a change in his expression. One day, Georgi suddenly leaped at his tormentor. Both boys crashed to the floorboards so hard that the boy's collarbone was broken! Perhaps even Georgi was startled by his own violence, for he never lost his temper again at the school.

When the other boys were filling their free time wrestling and joking, Georgi could be found lurking at the doors of the studios, observing more advanced classes. Older students such as Felia Doubrovska, who later came to the United States herself, noted his intent, intelligent little face as he peered in.

Georgi's keen observation of classes did not indicate love for ballet. He hated his hour-a-day class work. Why did he have to point all the muscles in his legs and feet so powerfully that they made long, strong lines? Who cared if his back was so straight that he looked like a noble young prince? At least steps that traveled diagonally from corner to corner of the studio were fun. One of these traveling steps that Georgi would have learned was *temps levée*, which was really a way of skipping, sending one leg out behind instead of bending it up in front. When Georgi pointed his legs with sudden strength in *temps levée*, he left the floor and felt for a split second as if he were flying. But he still saw no point in being stuck in dance class.

His afternoon academic classes were even worse. At least the boys and girls were together then, but Georgi could not be bothered to do well in French, math, and history; he only excelled in religion and music. Sometimes he would sit rubbing a bruise that arose because one of the dance teachers thumped his heavy ring against Georgi's legs when he made mistakes.

One girl, Alexandra Danilova, had entered the school the year before Georgi. She could tell there was something special about this shy, quiet, calm boy. Unlike Georgi, she loved the Imperial School. She loved being selected to participate in the productions of the great Maryinsky Theatre, where grand operas and ballets were produced for the Nobles of Russia. Imperial School children were put into these productions to fill out crowd scenes or to portray little servants. Only the best young students were chosen.

When he was about 10 years old, Georgi's turn came to be in his first ballet. He got to ride in one of the handsome carriages owned by Tsar Nicholas. The carriage took him and perhaps 10 other children from the Imperial School door to the Maryinsky Theatre door. To ride in the carriage, Georgi must have dressed in his school uniform: a handsome midnight blue wool jacket and slacks, with a dashing military-style hat. On the collar Georgi wore a golden pin shaped like a lyre, symbol of the performing arts. He didn't like ballet, but he did like his uniform.

The program that night was *The Sleeping Beauty*. Rehearsals had prepared Georgi to know when to go onstage, what to do there, how to exit, and where to go for his costume change. But nothing could have prepared him for the glories of a Maryinsky full-evening ballet production. Pyotr Ilyich Tchaikovsky's stirring, heart-wrenching music flowed over the slender boy waiting in the wings for his entrance. The tsar's treasury funded magnificent stage effects such as a tall, tumbling fountain, sheets of flame arising from nowhere, and an enchanted forest growing thickly as a fine boat sailed toward it across a shimmering lake. The world's most thrilling dancers leaped and turned for an audience that sat beneath sparkling chandeliers, amid walls decorated with white, gold, and peacock blue.

Suddenly Georgi was enthralled. The long boring class exercises had a reason to exist: to create this magnificence and beauty. And those powerful, graceful dancers onstage were his teachers! They had been Georgi's age at the Imperial School, years before. So

Georgi, if he kept working hard, might one day be like his favorite teacher, Samuel Andreyanov, who looked handsome as a god to Georgi that night.

Now he was excited.

Chapter 2
Surviving in Dangerous Soil (1914–1924)

The performing art that now gripped Georgi's soul was not a mere style of moving to music. Its roots lay in Italian martial arts training. Its evolution over four centuries into a performing art occurred across Europe through wars and international rivalry.

As the 1400s began, Europe was recovering from plagues and devastating conflicts. The peninsula called Italy was not one nation then. Instead, its people were organized into separate city-states: areas whose independent governments were centered in powerful cities. Rome, Florence, and Venice were three of the most powerful city-states.

These city-states found ways to interact without demolishing each other in war. The leaders of the city-states were what we would call *nobles*: they had traditions of educating themselves thoroughly, thinking before acting, structuring daily life with orderly purpose, and using courtesy to express ideas instead of anger and arguing. People with such patience and discipline aren't necessarily good people, but they can gain power and wealth.

Meanwhile, scholars in Italy were exploring fresh ideas. The plagues and wars had interfered with exchange of ideas among nations during the Middle Ages. Also, study of the Bible had dominated European thinking for centuries, and religious thinking had been the most highly regarded. Now emerging scientific discoveries, expanding world travel, and learning from other countries brought new inspiration to Italian culture. Intellectual freedom swept through Italy and spread northward into the rest of Europe. The European scholars felt their cultural and intellectual life was being reborn. Eventually this period was called the *Renaissance*, which means *rebirth*.

The Italian nobles participated eagerly in this exciting intellectual life. They applied their new sense of dignity and their inventiveness to their court manners—including the way they moved. Peasants slumped carelessly, walked or ran impulsively, and danced in wild crude formations. Nobles stood tall and elegant, walked with dignity, and danced socially in graceful, well-planned patterns.

Ballet movements come from the form of swordsmanship called fencing. Fencers' turned-out feet made swift changes of direction possible, while the curved, carefully placed arms enhanced balance and added grace. Men began to compete using the movement ideas in fencing, showing off with high, difficult leaps.

The Italian nobles liked to use their talents in music, poetry, and drama as part of feasts in which they displayed their intelligence and artistic achievements. They incorporated their movement ideas into these productions. Often they hired professional street jugglers and acrobats to generate ideas for their productions and supply extra movement training.

In 1453, a warrior named Mehmet II conquered the city of Constantinople, not far from Italy. Once known as Byzantium, this city contained manuscripts and art dating back to ancient Greece and Rome. The scholars of the city did not want to live under Mehmet II, so they fled to Italy. They showed their ancient works of learning to the universities of the Italian city-states.

Now the stories from ancient Greek and Roman myths became the new rage of the arts evenings. The stories were expressed in dances called *balleti*. Leonardo da Vinci was among the great artists who invented machinery to move painted scenery on and off the stage, or make performers appear and disappear.

Near the end of the 1400s, France claimed rights to areas in northern Italy. The ensuing wars and negotiations resulted in much intermarriage among French and Italian nobles. An Italian noblewoman, Caterina de' Medici, married the French king Henry II in 1533. As Catherine de Médicis, queen of France, she promoted the arts, in which she had been trained while growing up in Florence and Rome. In 1581, *Le Balet Comique de la Reine* (The Dramatic Artistic Full-Blown Production of the Queen) lasted for at least five hours and was viewed by as many as 10,000 people. It was produced by another Italian, Baldassarre Belgioioso, known to the French court as Balthazar de Beaujoyeuix. His written-out description (libretto) of this production was published throughout Europe, in the French language. Consequently, despite ballet's origin in Italy, the terms for ballet movements are known in their French form.

One hundred years later, ballet as an independent art had been standardized by one of the most creative, influential monarchs in European history: King Louis XIV of France. Under him, French culture became the most admired in Europe, and its art and styles were imitated across the European continent. He himself had performed ballets in his youth. He founded the official music and dance organization that became today's Paris Opéra.

By 1715, when Louis XIV died, the five basic positions of the arms and legs in ballet had been established by the ballet masters of the school he had established. This may not sound important, but in reality, ballet is an ingenious form of theme and variation. All ballet steps relate to one of the five positions (please see the illustrations at the end of the book). To assume a position according to its ballet ideal means to stand in a way that develops a long straight spine, and long, clean body lines. The most dizzying turns and high-flying leaps in ballet relate to the five positions and therefore retain their unified appearance of grace combined with power.

In 1738, Empress Anna of Russia established a ballet school in St. Petersburg. About 125 years later, French dancer and choreographer Marius Petipa became director, that is, ballet master, of the Russian Imperial School of Ballet as well as the Maryinsky Ballet. Strong-willed and energetic, Petipa dreamed up large, complex productions. He made Russian ballet flourish. Like ballet masters before him, he imported fine teachers, such as the Italian Enrico Cecchetti, and also topnotch dancers, such as the Italian ballerina Pierina Legnani.

Petipa wrote libretti (stories) and choreographed the dances for some of the most famous ballets in the world. The music for three of these ballets was composed by Pyotr Ilyich Tchaikovsky: *The Sleeping Beauty, Swan Lake*, and *The Nutcracker*. Petipa explained exactly how many minutes, even seconds, of music he needed for each section of the ballets he created, and Tchaikovsky composed gorgeous classical pieces that are still performed by orchestras all over the world. Petipa's choreography (enhanced in *Swan Lake* by his assistant, Lev Ivanov) established the ideal of classical ballet that still prevails now, more than a century later.

By the time Petipa died in 1899, ballet in France and Italy had deteriorated. Rich gentlemen came to leer at performances in which the dancers were almost all women, and women even played the men's parts. But in Denmark and Russia, men were still important to ballet, representing masculine ability and courtliness. Russian ballet was hailed as the best in the world. It was in this Russian ballet tradition that young Georgi Balanchivadze was trained after he entered the Imperial School in 1913.

Unfortunately, while Georgi, the little Russian potato, applied his artistic heart and forceful intelligence to becoming a dancer, the soil in which he was sprouting was changing composition.

The existence of the Imperial School and Maryinsky Ballet in St. Petersburg depended on tax money collected by the tsarist government (as did many hospitals, orphanages, homes for the blind, and other nonprofit Russian institutions). Outside Russia, World War I in 1914 began when Germany declared war on Serbia on behalf of Austria. Tsar Nicholas II then declared war on Germany on behalf of Serbia, and had to use tax money to train and equip soldiers. Meanwhile, inside Russia, Nicholas's government had long been challenged, especially by groups whose ideas were called *communism*: a government in which all money and property would be collected by a central authority and divided among all citizens in the national community equally. The most vocal and powerful communists were the Bolsheviks.

Inside the ballet school, the war only affected Georgi and his fellow students on Tuesdays, when they gave up sugar so the Russian troops could have enough. The school administrators carefully maintained the structured routine: meals, dance classes, academics, supervised entertainment and free time. The children felt protected and secure. As Alexandra Danilova later wrote, "Our education, our dance training, our lives would run their course, guided by the school. We proceeded from one day to the next, year after year, looking ahead sometimes but never worrying about the future. The routine carried us along on its own momentum" (1).

Georgi knew nothing of the efforts by communists to get rid of Tsar Nicholas II and set up their own government, an event known politically as a *revolution*. The nobles of Russia tried to ignore the revolutionaries. War afflicted Russia from without and revolution boiled within, but night after night in the Maryinsky Theatre, the operas, plays, and ballets went on.

After a ballet performance on December 6, 1916, the tsar's birthday, Tsar Nicholas gently handed 12-year-old Georgi and the other performing children each a tiny box of chocolates. Georgi gobbled them in private without dreaming of the frightening changes that would soon occur—changes that would not only transform the destiny to which he had looked forward, but affect his outlook on government for the rest of his life.

One Monday in mid-1917, gunshots blasted on Theatre Street, the cul-de-sac (short dead-end road) where the Imperial School stood. Danilova, foolishly curious at age 14, climbed the sill of one tall window and saw a man in uniform across the street take aim at her. The bullet that left a clean hole in the window glass missed her, and she ran to join the other students being herded into safer rooms by the school staff.

So began the October Revolution, the armed conflict that toppled Tsar Nicholas II's government in October 1917. The various communist groups, led by V. I. Lenin, united against the soldiers loyal to the tsar. Revolutionary troops flooded into the Imperial School one day, hunting for tsarist soldiers, but left after finding nothing but a lot of terrified ballet students. The communists sent the tsar and his family far away into the region of Russia called Siberia, where they were imprisoned in a house; eight months later, tsar and family were executed by gunshot.

The battling factions damaged the transportation systems that had developed between farms and cities. Even though the revolutionary government printed food coupons so everyone could eat for free, the coupons were useless because food became harder and harder to find. Without money from the tsar, the Imperial School could not buy fuel for heat, so Georgi and the other boys helped their schoolmasters rip up floorboards in the Theatre School's huge attic to burn for warmth and cooking. To conserve floorboards, the students continued their daily routine of class and rehearsal wearing shawls and gloves.

World War I was not quite over. Germans invaded St. Petersburg. The communist army threw them out, but supplies were more disrupted than before. Meanwhile, communist authorities decided ballet was a plaything of the hated Noble class, not a product of the people. The Imperial School of Theatre and Ballet was closed.

Georgi and the other students had to leave the school. They reunited with their anxious families. The honored life of the Maryinsky dancers as artists in the employ of the tsarist government ended. The theater was used as a venue for political speeches and the school as a barracks for revolutionary soldiers.

Meliton and Maria gave up the Lounatiokki house and moved back to St. Petersburg, which had been renamed Petrograd. When the revolutionary government appointed Meliton minister of culture to Georgia, the whole family except for Georgi and Aunt Nadia moved to the Georgian city of Tiflis.

Georgi remained with Aunt Nadia in case the ballet school reopened. This possibility seemed dim. World War II ended, and with it the German threat. But the communist groups were fighting not only tsarist defenders, but each other. Money that was needed to help common citizens eat instead went to feed soldiers and obtain weapons.

What does a 14-year-old boy do in a city whose citizens have to cook their pets to stay alive? Where a starving carthorse falls dead in the street and disappears within minutes under frantic kitchen knives?

Again Georgi acted rather than cowering in reaction. The piano playing that had made him so special at the Imperial School got him part-time work playing for silent films in rundown movie theaters. He also found odd jobs such as stitching canvas girths to saddles, or running messages. As payment, he received bits of food, or matches that he could trade for potato peelings. In desperation, he sometimes risked execution to steal fish from revolutionary army wharves in the cold darkness of Russian nights.

Repeatedly, at times shrinking into doorways to avoid bullets, Georgi and his friends drifted by the Imperial School, dreaming it might reopen. They likely had no idea that Anatole Lunacharsky, communist commissar of culture, loved ballet. Lunacharsky convinced the communist authorities that the performing arts were needed, to show the world the superiority of this new, ideal government.

All Georgi knew was that late in 1918, the school and theater reopened, supported by communist state funds. The Maryinsky, renamed the State Academic Theatre for Opera and Ballet, rehired the starving dancers. The hungry students returned. Their daily routine of classes and rehearsals resumed, as did their survival measures. They mixed coffee grounds with flour to make pancakes, ate horse feed, counted the boils on each other's skin while rationing the daily bread, and returned to cannibalizing the attic floor for wood.

These hardships showed the contrast between the communists' grand ideas—free public transportation, free food, free basic goods—versus the real after-effect of the October Revolution. Streetcars couldn't run without fuel, and the fuel supply lines were demolished. Local farms and local goods producers had been harmed or destroyed. The grand ideas had produced desperation, not abundance.

In Georgi's young mind, communism was an idea that plainly didn't work. Later in life, when he became an American citizen, the adult Balanchine always voted Republican because he viewed that party as anticommunist.

By 1920, the revolutionary government had stabilized. Its leading group, the Bolsheviks, had violently rebuffed all the other groups and established as its format a *soviet*, or council, that was supposed to hear and fulfill the needs of every citizen equally. An entire group of nations had been forced to support the Bolshevik government and form their own soviets, not as truly independent nations, but subject to the Bolshevik leaders, who called the whole enterprise the Union of Soviet Socialist Republics.

For a time, despite the harsh living conditions, a sense of revolutionary experimentation swept the arts world. Georgi eagerly observed performances of nontraditional ballet pieces by renowned ballet masters such as Mikhail Fokine. He again made himself special at the ballet school with piano playing: he accompanied dances for the end-of-year performances. Then he made himself even more special by choreographing something of his own.

Perhaps it was Georgi's innate daring that made him create a love pas de deux (dance for two) to Anton Rubenstein's *La Nuit* (The Night). He knew that the school's administrators guarded the students' sexual boundaries according to traditional ideals of purity. At the end of the dance, Georgi lifted his partner, student Olga Mungalova, over his head and carried her offstage as if she were a prize instead of escorting her off like a gentleman. *Unacceptable!* cried the administrators, except for the school's director, who announced that he wished the other students would show enough initiative to choreograph.

Fifty-nine years later, Soviet defector Mikhail Baryshnikov commented that *La Nuit* was still being performed at what had become the Kirov Ballet!

After *La Nuit*, Georgi began a four-year period of unbelievable activity. He found opportunities to choreograph for small concerts in parks and at charity benefits, earning a few more pennies for food. He graduated from the State School in 1921 at age 17 and became a member of the state ballet company (earning its painfully low salary). By then he had also enrolled in the music conservatory, where his brother Andrei had studied before going down to Georgia. Georgi's hope was to become a composer. He even composed a waltz that accompanied his own choreography of a duet with Alexandra Danilova, for which he received a favorable review in a paper.

He took every opportunity he could to perform and choreograph and so earn more. A pas de deux with 50-year-old Olga Preobrajenska earned him half a loaf of bread. A frantic 16-mile bike ride (he missed the train) got him in time to a performance with famed ballerina Elizaveta Gerdt. By now he was experiencing episodes of coughing in which he spit up blood, indicating possible exposure to the dangerous bacterial infection, tuberculosis, which attacks people who are undernourished and overtired.

Undernourished Georgi might be, but his physical misery was overridden by his inward creative urge. During this time he saw a performance by a Moscow-based dance company whose ballet master was Kasyan Goleizovsky. Goleizovsky's thoroughly untraditional presentation stripped away the customary elaborate costumes, leaving his dancers' bodies covered enough for decency, but free to move with flexibility and speed. Georgi was inspired with the courage to break Russian ballet's traditions in his own way.

Now he began a remarkable project called Evenings of the Young Ballet. About 15 dancers from the state ballet school and company gathered around him, sewing their own costumes and learning short pieces by Petipa, Fokine, and most of all, Georgi. Their young ballet master was quite different from the shy, serious child of years before. Throughout hours of intense work he cracked jokes without once expressing irritation or frustration. With his excited troupe he tacked up posters brashly advertising "The Evolution of Ballet: From Petipa through Fokine to Balanchivadze."

Having so small an advertising budget, he expected few people to seat themselves in the large round building called the Dumas for his show. But word of barefoot dancers and acrobatic lifts had spread. Hundreds of people, young and old, with a taste for experimentation or with anxiety about preserving tradition, filled the seats. As the evening progressed, cheers from some members of the audience decorated the air. Piercing whistles of disapproval from others set up a ruckus. No one reacted passively.

The next day, ballet historian and choreographer Akim Volynsky attacked Georgi in a newspaper review. Georgi responded in a newspaper called *Teatr* with a sarcastic article called "How Mr. Volynsky Flogged Himself." A photo of Georgi with long slicked-down hair and dark, brooding eyes accompanied the photo.

Common consensus in the arts world is that whether a new piece is loved or hated is fine; the one reaction that terrifies artists is indifference. St. Petersburg was not indifferent to Georgi's work at all. Good and bad opinions circulated vigorously. Meanwhile, he produced another Evening of the Young Ballet, against the approval of the authorities of either the state ballet school or the dance company. In fact, the dancers were forbidden to participate in Georgi's productions unless they received special permission . . . which did not materialize.

Georgi, now 19, kept educating himself by attending exhibitions of music, dance, and art, thirsting for new ideas. He married Tamara Gevergeva, age 16, a singer who had belatedly joined the ballet school after the revolution, and who danced in Georgi's productions. More and more, Georgi and other artists found that Soviet authorities were squelching truly revolutionary ideas.

Early in 1924, when Georgi was barely 20, the October Revolution's main leader, Vladimir Lenin, died. In the face of the ensuing political unrest, choreographer Mikhail Fokine and famed dancers such as Olga Preobrajenska, Matilda Kchessinskaya, Olga Spessivtseva, and Tamara Karsavina left Russia.

Fear entered the remaining dancers. They avoided soldiers and anyone involved in politics, never knowing who was spying on whom. Everyone was concerned when Danilova's best friend, Lydia Ivanova, became girlfriend to a Soviet soldier, but she paid no attention to Danilova's cautioning.

In spring of 1924, former opera baritone Vladimir Dimitriev convinced Commissar Lunacharsky to let him take a small crowd of dancers and musicians on a tour of Europe to display Soviet artistic superiority. Dimitriev asked Georgi, his wife Gevergeva, Danilova and her friend Ivanova, and a male dancer named Nicholas Efimov to participate. All five said yes.

Nervously, the performers awaited their exit visas. Ivanova was even more nervous about traveling on an ocean liner than about her visa, because a fortune teller had predicted she would die on water. One night, she did not return to her room at the school. The next day, the dancers learned she had taken a short ferry ride with her soldier boyfriend. Somehow, she and three men got knocked overboard. The three men were rescued, but Ivanova drowned. Her horrified friends felt sure her death had been arranged by someone who feared she might gain access to government secrets through the boyfriend.

When the exit visas were granted in mid-June, the dancers could not pack their costumes and meager personal belongings fast enough. With Dimitriev and a few musicians they boarded a steamship and headed across the Baltic Sea to a German port—well beyond Soviet borders.

Chapter 3
Apollo: Blooming Triumphantly in Diaghilev's Garden (1924–1928)

Four gaunt young Russian dancers and their agent were treated to a miracle as they entered the ship's dining room: *rolls*! Baskets full on every table, beside dishes of gleaming butter! No guards stood threateningly by to enforce rations. Tears sprang to Georgi's eyes—they had all half-starved for seven years—but the tears vanished as the group sat down and tucked napkins under their chins.

They gobbled free bread and butter with their meals for two and a half days. Upon landing in Germany, they discovered that free bread with meals was the custom there, and they hid extra rolls in their napkins to take back to their hotel rooms.

They traveled from Stettin, on Germany's coast, inland to Berlin. Dimitriev got busy trying to book shows. Georgi had his long, thick hair cut, and could then buy a hat that fit. Danilova minced out of a cheap clothing shop thrilled with her purchase of a glitzy purple sweater.

Before Dimitriev even booked one performance, a telegram from the Soviet government arrived demanding that the touring group return home. The musicians obeyed. The dancers, by silent agreement, stayed put. It was already clear to Georgi that he was unlikely to see his family again, whether he returned to the Soviet Union or not. And Germany had food. No, Dimitriev and his four dancers, with their few hand-sewn costumes, kept their Berlin hotel rooms.

Their new lives as Soviet exiles had few thrills at first. Dimitriev booked several weeks' worth of shows in out-of-the-way spots in Germany, and then got a month's vaudeville work at the Empire Theatre in London. But in two weeks the Empire Theatre dismissed the troupe: their costume changes were too slow and ballet didn't spark its audiences.

The group's visas would expire in two weeks. They would all have to return . . . oh, no . . .

To various degrees, the group gave way to short-tempered exclamations and tears. Georgi alone kept calm, as if sure something better would come. A few days later, the five received a life-changing telegram from some guy they'd barely heard of named Serge Diaghilev.

Come to Paris and audition for my company, Les Ballets Russe, was the essence of the telegram's message.

Might as well, decided the dancers. It was either that or return to friendly Petrograd. Not.

Dimitriev got them all from London across the English channel and into the capital city of France. The dancers had heard of Les Ballets Russes. They knew that a former Maryinsky danseur (male dancer) named Vaslav Nijinsky, one of the most fascinating dancers the ballet world has ever known, had performed and choreographed for Diaghilev. So had another Maryinsky star named Anna Pavlova, who subsequently booked her own tours throughout Europe, the United States, and Cuba; she was most famous for her solo called *The Dying Swan*. Also, several prominent dancers and choreographers had left the Soviet Union to join this Ballets Russes.

The dancers with Dimitriev were directed to the mansion of Diaghilev's friend Misia Sert, wife of famed Spanish painter José Sert, where they were led into a large room. There sat a portly middle-aged man. He had almond-scented hair that was dyed jet black except for one white stripe combed back in a wave from his forehead. He wore a monocle and false teeth. He asked the dancers to show what they could do. Twenty-one-year-old Danilova scoffed at the idea of having to dance in audition mode, as if any Maryinsky dancer could be less than what Diaghilev needed! But when Diaghilev quietly insisted, she complied along with the others. One of Diaghilev's lower false teeth showed in a little smile of approval.

Next he asked Georgi an odd question: Could the 20-year-old choreograph opera ballets *very* fast? Georgi had set only one opera dance for a small company back in St. Petersburg, but he daringly answered yes. Diaghilev nodded and left.

The dancers waited a week in a hotel room while their tiny cash pile shrank. At last Diaghilev offered a performance contract to all four, which they eagerly accepted—but rehearsals and paychecks would not begin for a month, and they only had cash for another thrifty week. Resourceful Georgi saved the day by selling the one thing of value that he owned: his best suit.

Back to London they went because Les Ballets Russes was rehearsing there. Diaghilev handed Georgi a new challenge: take a day's rehearsal and teach several Ballets Russes dancers, all older and more experienced than he, a sample of his choreography. Georgi stepped to the front of the studio and started setting a piece he had done for the Evenings of the Young Ballet called *March Funèbre*. The Ballets Russes dancers learned the unfamiliar movements, reluctantly impressed by Georgi's imperturbable confidence. At the end of the day, Diaghilev returned, viewed what Georgi had accomplished, and silently disappeared. Had he liked what he saw? No one knew.

A few days later, company choreographer Bronislava Nijinska concluded her long period of discontent by leaving for good. Diaghilev announced that the new ballet master of Les Ballets Russes was Georgi Melitonovich Balanchivadze. It was winter 1925. The new ballet master had just turned 21.

Almost immediately, Diaghilev simplified Georgi's name to George Balanchine—Russian-sounding enough to credit him as an authentic Maryinsky dancer, but simpler for European audiences to pronounce. Tamara's last name was shortened from Gevergeva to Geva. Danilova's and Efimóv's names stayed the same.

The first thing the four noticed about their new company was that it was small (only 40 dancers) compared to the 200-member Maryinsky/State Theatre company. The second thing was that, though its lead performers were outstanding, its corps dancers' work was sloppy. Ever since the October Revolution seven years before, excellent dancers from Russia had become less and less available and Diaghilev had to hire a less competent crew.

The third thing was that the company did not want Balanchine as their ballet master. Its dancers were loyal to Nijinska, despite her temperamental moods, and they resented this youngster. But their dislike melted swiftly because Balanchine was so pleasant to work with. Former choreographer Léonide Massine had often worked in a cloud of gloom, Nijinska had bouts of depression, and once when Mikhail Fokine lost his temper (again), he threw chairs. By contrast, in the words of Diaghilev soloist Ninette de Valois, Balanchine displayed "easy brilliance, strong individualism, humor, and a rare intelligence"—not to mention unfailing courtesy (2).

Only as the days passed did Balanchine and his wife and friends realize how fortunate they were to land a Ballets Russes contract. Diaghilev wasn't just a fat old man with dyed hair, fur collar, and top hat. He was one of the most educated and well-regarded people in Europe. Fluent in French as well as Russian, he had studied piano, music composition, visual art, and law in his youth. He had produced head-turning art shows and operas in Russia before starting Les Ballets Russes in 1909. He became a true impresario: a person who could assemble the dancers, visual artists, musicians, composers, stage personnel, and funding to mount fresh, artistically superb performances.

Many prominent men and women in Europe were interested in being arts patrons—donating to support excellent art—just as their ancestors had been more than 400 years before. They trusted Diaghilev with their money, and he rewarded them by finding the most talented, avant-garde (forward-thinking) artists in Europe. No less than the likes of Pablo Picasso and Henri Matisse designed and painted sets and costumes. Such fiery composers as Richard Strauss and Igor Stravinsky composed tradition-breaking music. The world's most renowned Russian dancers and choreographers took care of the dancing. Les Ballets Russes at that point was the most prestigious ballet company in the world.

It was quickly evident that Diaghilev had his flaws. He could be cuttingly unkind if he felt insulted or was disappointed by one of the artists he had employed. He had a damaging health problem called diabetes; he should have stuck to a diet low in sugar and alcohol, but he didn't. Also, he did not always keep his personal life adequately separated from his work. For example, he had embroiled young Vaslav Nijinsky in a homosexual love affair. When Nijinsky married a ballerina named Romola de Pulszky in 1913, Diaghilev jealously fired them both.

In 1925, Diaghilev was older and wiser. Keeping Les Ballets Russes in existence through World War I had been difficult. Patrons had donated but also had given him loans, and after the war ended, Diaghilev had heavy debts. But he kept Les Ballets Russes in business, and made sure his dancers got paid before he paid himself. Danilova later wrote, "He taught us that nobody works for free, and that if they do, there is no control: you have no authority over someone who is doing you a favor" (3). Few life lessons are as important as that one.

Diaghilev remembered that Balanchine and the other dancers were young—college age. He encouraged all the dancers to keep educating themselves. He took Balanchine with him to Italy along with his right-hand man, Boris Kochno, and Serge Lifar, a gifted young male dancer. In the famed galleries of the Uffizi museum, the younger men saw, expressed through visual art, that same profound essence that Balanchine had heard in music and seen in ballet. Diaghilev insisted that they all study paintings carefully to learn principles of visual design that applied to arranging groups onstage.

And Diaghilev helped maintain discipline. He himself liked to sleep late, but one day he suddenly decided to get up and watch morning rehearsal. That particular day, young Balanchine had let the dancers out early, because the day was lovely and the rehearsal studio was in the gloomy basement of the opera house. Diaghilev arrived to an empty studio, looked around, and left. He did not mention this later to Balanchine. However, the opera house personnel did.

Balanchine took the hint and never cheated rehearsal time again.

Balanchine soon found out why Diaghilev had placed that query about *very* fast opera ballet choreography. One important asset to paying Ballets Russes bills was a contract with the Princess of Monaco. (Monaco is a tiny nation with a gorgeous resort area on France's south coast.) This contract stated that in addition to producing ballet concerts for several months of the year, Les Ballets Russes would do the dances in Monaco's operas. (These dances were a holdover from the Renaissance combinations of drama, music, and dance.) Operas were produced frequently in Monaco. Most had a dance interlude. During the two-month 1925 opera season Balanchine set an impressive 12 opera ballets.

What was impressive about his doing so? Firstly, in Russia he had never choreographed for more than about 15 dancers. These operas in Monaco often involved all 40 Ballets Russes members, and Balanchine had to develop floor patterns (traffic patterns) so that dancers would neither bump into each other while rapidly and forcefully crossing the stage, nor smack each other when they moved their arms and legs. Also, Balanchine had to divide the dancers into logical yet interesting groups. Their movements had to coordinate visually and also fit the music. It takes a lot longer than 2 minutes of rehearsal to produce 2 usable minutes of choreography, and opera ballets can last 20 minutes. So Balanchine was indeed producing *very* fast.

Another impressive aspect was that Balanchine wasn't familiar with all these operas. He had to learn the music, often by reading the score. Listening to the radio or a scratchy phonograph helped, but there were no CDs, mp3s, or handheld electronic devices—certainly not the Internet! Here Georgi's love of music and disciplined training came in very handy. Unlike previous Ballets Russes choreographers, he could play sections of the music himself in rehearsal on the piano. He explained how to count the beats in the music so the dancers could time their steps and be ready for their cues. The dancers were grateful, because music rehearsed on a piano can sound quite different from the same music played by an orchestra. Balanchine made the dancers feel much more secure about hearing their cues and matching steps to notes in performance.

Balanchine used the opera music to teach himself about choreography. He later commented that from opera composer Giuseppe Verdi, he learned how to make soloists and groups dance and rest so the choreographic ideas were clear. The dancers, usually bored by portraying village folk or temple worshipers for operas, enjoyed the constant variety Balanchine managed to inject into the pieces.

As part of the Monaco contract, Les Ballets Russes also produced full evenings of ballet. An early choreographic assignment for Balanchine was a piece called *Le chant du rossignol*—The Song of the Nightingale. Famed composer Igor Stravinsky had written its swift-running orchestral score and its haunting, weird melodies. Balanchine could translate its elusive counts into fascinating dance patterns. However, he needed a suitable dancer to be the nightingale. Even young, sparky Danilova looked too substantial to portray a tiny bird.

One of the Ballets Russes men, Anton Dolin, suggested a 14-year-old girl named Alicia Marks, whom he had seen training in London. Balanchine and Diaghilev hired her after a rigorous audition. They were thrilled at seeing adult-level technique in such a slight, slender body—she was perfect. She could even do *fouetté* turns traveling forward and backward diagonally, oscillating her arms in swim-like strokes to look like a hopping little bird. The difficulty of such a maneuver can only be understood by those with enough training to try it.

Alicia, whose last name was changed to Markova, moved to Paris with a governess. As performance time approached, she broke down in tears because her costume was white, and nightingales are brown. With the subtle coaxing of a big brother, Balanchine convinced her to wear it.

Balanchine's choreography to *Le chant* was well received. And when Markova fluttered forth from her stage-prop cage, her delicate strength was an instant hit with the Monaco audience.

A quite different effect resulted the night a virus made her too ill to dance. Absolutely no one knew her role—except Balanchine.

Perhaps this was one time that Balanchine was glad he was only five feet eight inches tall and still quite slim, for in a hastily improvised costume he was able to cram his 140 pounds into the cage built for the 80-pound Markova. The curtain rose, and right on cue, he squeezed out of the cage door and fluttered muscularly through the ultra-feminine steps he himself had set. Watching from a box seat, Diaghilev collapsed with silent laughter.

The Princess of Monaco happened to attend. She was heard to comment later that Mr. Balanchine did well, but she preferred Miss Markova.

As Balanchine proceeded to his next new ballet, the dancers' lives assumed a rhythm much like their Imperial School days. At 9:00 A.M. they sweated through a demanding class taught by Enrico Cecchetti. Morning rehearsal ran for another hour and a half. Next they ate lunch, rested, sewed ribbons or elastic on new ballet shoes or did other personal chores, or had extra rehearsals. By 6:00 P.M. they were at the theater warming up, adjusting costumes, and putting on makeup. They also assessed irregularities such as how much the opera singers might be crowding the dance space, or whether choreography had to be changed to cover for sick or injured dancers. By the time they performed, ate a late meal, and tumbled into bed, midnight had slipped by. Nine o'clock in the morning found them once again at Master Cecchetti's barre.

Balanchine performed actively, learning standard Ballets Russes repertory as well as dancing in his own pieces. With his high brow, eagle nose, and slight build, he was more a *demi-caractère* dancer than a leading-man type; as a comical minstrel in blackface, or as the evil magician Kastchei in *Swan Lake*, he excelled. But he also commanded respect in straightforward roles.

His paycheck was almost twice what the other dancers got because he was paid also as ballet master. He earned it. While other dancers rested in the afternoons, he attended planning meetings for new ballets with Diaghilev, the stage manager, the composer, the librettist (usually Boris Kochno), and the set and costume designers. He learned new music. He tried to recruit more dancers from the Soviet Union for a while; but the Soviet government interfered with the communication and no new dancers came.

Balanchine also insisted that he, Geva, Danilova, and Efimov pool one-fourth of each of their salaries to support Dimitriev. The man was not needed to book shows any more, but he had, after all, gotten them out of the Soviet Union and they were still his only source of personal income.

The Ballets Russes dancers were together most hours of the day and night, seven days a week. They had to get along well. Jealousy or misunderstanding might set tempers flaring, but Diaghilev would not tolerate smoldering conflict and the dancers learned to resolve the difficulties—or find another job.

In the midst of performances, planning meetings, and setting a hilarious slapstick dance called *Barabau,* Balanchine found his marriage bond with Geva loosening. Geva considered herself not only a ballet dancer, but a stage singer needing singing opportunities; Balanchine at this time was all about ballet. Geva wanted to go out and see Monaco night life after performing on some nights. Balanchine preferred to stay home, and they quarreled.

Neither Geva at age 19 nor Balanchine at age 22 seemed to know how to care for their marriage, which is not hard to understand. Who had their models been as they grew up? Their over-pressured (and in Balanchine's case, absent) parents? Soviet Union activists who advocated abolishing traditional family structure? Dancers like Kchessinskaya who had multiple love affairs? At least Samuel Andreyanov and Elizaveta Gerdt had a solid marriage, but when they taught in the Imperial School the subject was ballet, not relational counseling. Balanchine's education in the arts was world-class, but he was left poorly prepared to endure the personal growth needed for the close covenant of marriage.

He did not speak to anyone of his problems with Geva. Instead, he began to pay obvious attention to Danilova, who felt so embarrassed, she even considered returning to the Soviet Union to help Balanchine and Geva's marriage survive. But by summer 1926, Geva herself moved out. She had decided to leave Ballets Russes and perform with a theater group called Chauve-Souris. Though she was hurt by the breakdown of her personal relationship with Balanchine, the working relationship she had with him remained friendly. In fact, he set several short solos for her to use for auditions and nightclub acts before she left.

This odd juncture of an ended romance with an ongoing artistic relationship was a pattern that persisted throughout Balanchine's life.

Danilova had always harbored romantic feelings for Balanchine. Once Geva left, Danilova envisioned a fine church wedding with him. Unfortunately, his marriage papers were in Petrograd. He could not obtain a legal divorce from Geva, so he could not have an official marriage to Danilova. He wanted her nonetheless to move in and live with him as his wife. If she wouldn't, he told her, he would take a job in America. Weeping, unable to imagine life without him, she agreed.

Diaghilev did not agree. Amid the wagging tongues of the Ballets Russes personnel, Diaghilev summoned Balanchine for a two-hour conversation behind closed doors. Balanchine emerged looking solemn but unruffled. He refused to tell Danilova what he and Diaghilev had said, but somehow the impresario and everyone else accepted their unofficial union, and life at the Ballets Russes moved on.

Balanchine's packed schedule of producing new ballets while also performing continued. Like all Maryinsky students, he had learned social dances and internationally known folk dances as well as ballet. Any of these styles might show up in his choreography. Diaghilev criticized Balanchine at times for showing great beauty in one section of a ballet and then ending it in a thoughtlessly different manner. But generally the impresario encouraged and respected his ballet master.

Early in 1927, Balanchine landed from a jump in rehearsal and collapsed to the floor with white-hot pain in one knee. Dancers commonly suffer one or more lesser injuries during a performing season because no one can jump, twist, and bend hundreds of times a day without stress to joints and muscles. Ballet training strengthens bodies and shows how to avoid accidents—but weariness or an irregular surface can mean serious trouble. In Balanchine's case, his knee required surgery and a month in a cast. Upon recovery he found that his knee could not support him through a rigorous performance. He was limited to character roles that did not demand high ballet technique.

With his usual don't-look-back-or-mope attitude, Balanchine said, "Good! Now I won't have to work so hard" (4). He applied himself to developing better choreography.

His decisive push forward was about to carry him from being a good choreographer to being a great one.

For Balanchine, whose life from infancy was filled with melody and harmony, choreography was ruled by music. For him, preparing for a ballet started with listening to music for ideas; or it started with an idea for which he found someone to compose the music, in which case he considered the resulting ballet not to be his alone, but one in collaboration with the composer. In his own book written in middle age, *Balanchine's Complete Stories of the Great Ballets*, he commented that, to prepare for a ballet, "I study the score and listen to it. If a piano transcription of the score exists, I play the piece *over and over* [emphasis added] on the piano; if it does not exist, I make a transcription myself." No wonder he was later to remark, "Often I spend much more time learning a score than I do working out a ballet" (5).

By the time Balanchine clapped his hands and said, "We begin," to start a rehearsal, he had made the music of his ballet a part of himself. He did not work out choreographic diagrams and steps ahead of time. Instead, he led a dancer by the hand to a spot on the broad studio floor and stood quietly a moment. He next demonstrated a movement idea (carefully, for the sake of his knee), and the dancer would try it. If his idea didn't work, he modified it to be, not less difficult, but more fitting to the dancer's individual ability. Thus Balanchine's choreography had an exciting, on-the-spot sense of discovery for both him and his dancers. What he set for one superb lead dancer might not fit another's body shape or particular strength, and he changed solos as needed for dancers who alternated in the same roles—always producing combinations of steps that seemed to grow from the music itself.

Composers also benefited from Balanchine's musicality. One, Vladimir Dukelsky (known later in America as Vernon Duke), contrasted choreographer Léonide Massine's collaboration unfavorably to that of Balanchine and Diaghilev. Dukelsky said Balanchine could actually improvise music similar to what he needed, and Diaghilev could at least describe the projected musical ideas. Massine, however provided little to no guidance. Under him, the composing process was frustratingly hit-and-miss.

Balanchine respected all composers, but there was one whom he revered: Igor Stravinsky. Balanchine had heard Stravinsky's pieces played back in St. Petersburg, and dreamed of setting a ballet to a Stravinsky score. *Le chant du rossignol* had given him that chance. He was thrilled when Stravinsky, almost a quarter-century Balanchine's senior, expressed complete satisfaction with Balanchine's understanding of the score and with his choreography.

Now a finer opportunity yet appeared. Diaghilev wanted to produce another Stravinsky piece: *Apollon Musagète* (Apollo, Leader of the Muses).

As a composer, Stravinsky was profoundly inventive—thrillingly so. His work revealed important ideas to his listeners, including ideas they did not necessarily like. Ballets Russes had sparked a small riot at Paris's Théâtre des Champs-Élysées in 1913 when it premiered Stravinsky's evening-length piece *Le sacre du printemps* (The Rite of Spring). In its driving, urgent rhythms and orchestral bellows and shrieks, Stravinsky's music harked back to Russia's most primitive history. Vaslav Nijinsky's nonballetic choreography depicted the sacrifice of a village maiden to Russia's primitive gods. Many audience members, who wanted to see complex civilized ideas rather than crude primitive behavior, began to roar their disapproval. Audience supporters of the ballet responded angrily, fistfights broke out, and police had to be called in at intermission to restore order. Though the audience remained in their seats for the rest of the performance, they kept whistling, booing, or shouting bravo throughout, according to which side they were on. (Subsequent audiences were calmer.)

Stravinsky's other work ranged from disturbing to unspeakably beautiful, and Balanchine loved it all. Deep within both Stravinsky and Balanchine was a gift for reaching beyond Western civilization's idealized self-perception, and expressing everything from raw instinct to the noblest ideals of beauty and truth.

Stravinsky's *Apollon Musagète* paid tribute to these nobler ideals. Its subject was a god of the ancient Greeks: Apollo, god of the sun, prophecy, justice, help to the needy, crop growth, music, poetry, and all the arts. Apollo was served by muses: nine supernatural women through whom he inspired humans to artistic expression. He was a figure of glory in Greek thinking.

Stravinsky produced a sound of ancient simplicity, peace, and strength through careful artistic selection: for this piece, stringed instruments only. Furthermore, he used only the diatonic scale (meaning only the seven notes of a major scale, as when C major scale is played on all white keys on the piano). He had written the piece a year before, in 1927, so Balanchine had a complete score to work with from the start. As always, Balanchine read the orchestral score thoroughly and also played repeatedly through the piano transcription.

As had occurred so long ago on the piano bench in Lounatiokki at age 7—and again on the Maryinsky stage at age 10—through *Apollon Musagète* Balanchine suddenly saw art in a blaze of new light. He realized that Stravinsky had not *limited* himself by composing *Apollon* only with strings and the diatonic scale. Rather, he had *freed* himself to choose only those instruments and musical notes that would unite the music completely with the grand story of Apollo. The result was a musical piece with singular, particular impact.

At that moment, the 24-year-old ballet master understood: He, too, was free to consider the many movements and gestures that poured through his mind, and eliminate what did not fit. He, too, could discover the laws of artistic unity. He could create dances with the focused impact of a Stravinsky masterpiece.

A sense of daring flooded him. He could hardly wait for the first *Apollon* rehearsals.

The moment was perfect. He had worked for three years with Diaghilev's dancers. He and they knew each other's abilities. The characters in *Apollon Musagète* were Apollo and three muses, and the cast members were highly achieved artists. Apollo was danced by Serge Lifar, the young Russian man who had started classical training in his middle teens. Starting so late meant Lifar's body did not develop the flowing lines and turnout of a classical dancer, but he was handsome, he worked hard, and he emanated an electrifying presence onstage. Lubov Tchernicheva danced Calliope, muse of poetry; then 38 years old, she was a graduate of the Imperial School and had danced with Diaghilev for 17 years. Gorgeous, long-legged Felia Doubrovska performed Polyhymnia, muse of mime. Two ballerinas alternated in the role of Terpsichore, muse of dance: Alicia Nikitina, who was yet another Imperial School graduate, and Alexandra Danilova.

Abetted by Stravinsky's presence and encouragement, *Apollon Musagète* took shape. Balanchine kept the costumes simple and used the muses' long, flexible limbs to make remarkable designs as the three surrounded Apollo. Lifar's steps reflected the self-controlled passion and lordly play of the young Apollo, whom Balanchine depicted being born, emerging into an understanding of who he was, dancing with the muses, and then leading them all to Mount Olympus, home of the gods.

Lifar, however, presented a problem. The pure lines of ballet fitted Apollo ideally, but Lifar's body lines did not fit the ballet ideal. Turned-out classical steps emphasized his inflexible hips and bowed legs. Balanchine decided to use the toes-turned-forward look he had experimented with in *Marche Funèbre*. As the dancers moved through the combinations, Balanchine had them alternate standing high on half-toe (Lifar) or on pointe shoes (the women), and then standing flat-footed, rocking heel to toe. He added arm positions with bent angles and flat hands instead of ballet's shoulder-through-fingertip curve. The visual result harked back to the images in ancient Greek art.

Whenever a strong new idea appears, it gets re-used and imitated. In *Apollon Musagète*, Balanchine had introduced a new idea about how to use classical ballet. He re-used the idea himself many times, and many choreographers imitated it. Eventually Balanchine's style came to be known as *neoclassical* (new classical). Diaghilev thought so highly of it that he compared it to the pure classicism established by Petipa for the Maryinsky Ballet.

On June 12, 1928, the ballet premiered at the Théâtre Sarah Bernhardt in Paris. Stravinsky himself conducted the orchestra. The audience reaction must have reminded Stravinsky and Diaghilev of the *Sacre* premiere 15 years before. Murmurs of approval and disapproval rippled through the crowd. As the ballet progressed, the audience tension mounted. Onstage, the dancers were conscious that they were making history. They knew they were presenting something great, even though cries of "Boo!" could be heard amid applause as the ballet concluded.

Noted actor-producer Gordon Craig loved *Apollon* so much, he left at intermission to keep its impression undiluted. The mixed ideas the other audience members had about Apollo showed up in their subsequent reactions. One arts critic demanded of Balanchine, "When did anyone ever see Apollo on his knees?" Balanchine retorted, "When did anyone ever see Apollo?" (6). Some newspaper critics demeaned *Apollon*; others hailed it as a landmark collaboration between choreographer and composer.

Lifar's Apollo earned a kiss on the leg from Diaghilev, with the reminder that the impresario had kissed no dancer's leg since Vaslav Nijinsky had covered the stage in one leap in *Le spectre de la rose* in 1911. Balanchine received no kiss. For him, such a gesture would have seemed ridiculous. He knew what he had accomplished. The popularity of *Apollo* in ballet repertories the world over has not faded in more than 80 years.

Chapter 4
Prodigal Son: From Earthquake to New Roots **(1928–1934)**

While other ballet companies started imitating the partnering ideas Balanchine had introduced in *Apollon Musagète*, he was inventing more. In *Le Bal* (The Ball), for example, he had Danilova rise on pointe, crouch into a deep knee bend while still on pointe, then spring into the air for Anton Dolin to catch her against his chest, her back arched away from him.

What was so important about this bit of invention? The importance was that Dolin wasn't just holding Danilova's hand to maintain her balance so she could do slow turns and balances on pointe. This showed how Balanchine didn't just repeat the partnering ideas the Imperial School had taught him—ideas that had developed in the 19th century, when dance audiences were fascinated with women dancing on the tips of their toes without harming their feet. A man holding the woman's hand to balance her while she did even harder steps on pointe had extended that fascination in a new direction. Now Balanchine extended pas de deux from man-support-woman into a dialogue between man and woman, changing the very nature of what partnering had been. Danilova commented that under Balanchine, "[T]he adagio would be more like a dance, conveying a mood. The man and woman create something together" (7).

Balanchine also extended ballet technique to match his ideas. Russian ballet training had frowned upon having the legs lifted above waist level. Such moves were for tasteless circus performers. Ballet, by contrast, had dignity. Balanchine, however, shrugged off tradition and encouraged his dancers to develop their flexibility beyond traditional limitations—and made history again in another ballet that starred Serge Lifar.

This ballet, *Le fils prodigue* (The Prodigal Son), made Ballets Russes history as well as ballet history. By early 1929, Balanchine had choreographed a range of ballets for Diaghilev, many of which have not been mentioned in this book, but all of which emphasized modern ideas, downplayed sentiment, and avoided religion. Suddenly Diaghilev got fed up with his own hunt for whatever was different and untraditional. He decided to do a story from the New Testament.

The story of the prodigal son is meant to show God's unfailing compassion when faced with human wrongdoing. It appears in the Gospel of Luke, chapter 15. A young man decides he doesn't want to wait until his father dies to get his share of the inheritance; he wants it now. While his older brother watches in disgust, their father gives the younger son the money. The young man leaves and wastes his father's gift on fancy parties and prostitutes. Penniless and able to find work only caring for pigs, he decides to go home, beg his father's forgiveness, and ask to be returned to his father's household—as a hired man, for he feels unfit to be treated as a son. However, the father sees him arriving and runs to meet him. Jubilant when the son asks his forgiveness, the father orders a feast. The angry older son wants the younger one to get what he deserves, but the father is so glad that his son is now willing to live a good life, he refuses to punish him.

Diaghilev had spent 20 years producing music and dance that appealed to ideals and intellect. He cautioned his dancers against oozy displays of feeling. Yet he now commissioned well-known composer Serge Prokofiev to write music that would reflect deep human emotion. French painter Georges Rouault, famous for religious themes, designed sets and costumes. And Balanchine— renowned for containing his own emotions, and producer of the regal, superhuman *Apollo*—began the choreography.

To focus on the issue between son and father, Boris Kochno's libretto eliminated the older brother and the pig farm scene. Now Balanchine unleashed his imagination in new directions. One example was his use of an importance piece of Rouault's set: a many-legged table. Balanchine had this table on its back in the first scene to represent the fence around the Father's house. The Son leaped over this fence to depart to the town. In the next scene, the set piece was a tavern table that the tavern Revelers lifted and manipulated. At one point the Son was thrust suddenly into the air while on the table, terrified as the Revelers bullied him. At another point, the Siren who seduced him (danced by Felia Doubrovska) stood atop the table held at a high slant, glaring triumphantly as the wasted Son groveled on the floor.

Throughout the Siren-Son pas de deux, Balanchine used Doubrovska's long legs and circus-performer flexibility. At one point she climbed the Son's body, wrapped herself backward around him like a huge belt, slid from his chest to the floor, and entwined his arms and legs into hers. Thus the entanglement of uncontrolled desires was memorably symbolized.

Balanchine did not forget the revelation about unity of gesture. Besides the circus-like moves for the Revelers and the Siren, the Son's solos were full of leaps that used ballet's intense leg-pointing, yet were not traditionally balletic. When at the end the Son approached his Father, Balanchine decided the Son would not even dance on his feet. Instead, he would clasp his hands behind his back and inch on his knees across the stage. Instead of having the Father rush to the Son as in the biblical parable, the Father would wait, staff held sternly to one side, other hand clasping the edge of his cloak. The Son would reach him and clamber up his legs, then curl against his chest in humiliated appeal. As Balanchine worked out the final moments of the music, he decided the Father would throw his cloak around the Son in a gesture of eternal protectiveness and the curtain would then fall.

Prokofiev, the composer, had been away from Paris while *Prodigal Son* took shape. He returned and saw one of the ballet's final rehearsals. He hated it except for the final scene and expressed his disgust openly. When Balanchine later asked if Prokofiev would share royalties from *Prodigal Son*'s performances, as Stravinsky had shared royalties from *Apollon Musagète*, Prokofiev screamed at him to get out. Awed by this famous middle-aged composer, Balanchine apologized for mentioning the matter. But he never choreographed Prokofiev music again.

Not quite a year after the premiere of *Apollon Musagète*, on May 20, 1929, *Le fils prodigue* also premiered at the Théâtre Sarah Bernhardt. Many in the audience wept freely when the Father's cloak at last embraced Lifar, and no boos were mixed into the pro-longed applause and cheers that met the performers as they bowed. Backstage, a teary-eyed Diaghilev told Balanchine this was his best ballet yet.

With this rich new ballet, the company went on its London tour, which concluded July 26, 1929. The dancers were scheduled to tour until August 4, but Diaghilev had to go to Venice, so he gathered them backstage to say farewell until fall. As had often been the case, his cheeks were pale as bread dough, and his eyes glittered from within dark circles as he quietly thanked the dancers. He remarked that the entire performance schedule for next season was already set—a first for the Ballets Russes. He then kissed Danilova on the cheek and left. The dancers did not worry about his labored walk and low voice; he had looked awful before and then been fine the next day.

After the tour, an excited Balanchine returned to England with Anton Dolin. The two men plus a former Diaghilev dancer named Lydia Lopokova were to appear in a movie! It was called *Dark Red Roses*. Balanchine had choreographed a dance sequence for the three of them. The filming was scheduled on August 19, 1929. On that day, Lopokova sat on the set in her white dress beside Dolin and Balanchine, both men in pirate pants and deep brown makeup. Filming was behind schedule, so they sat and sat, into the night. At last a news vendor went by and Dolin bought a paper because he glimpsed a picture of Serge Diaghilev on the front page. Dolin wondered happily what new waves the impresario was making now—and then his eyes widened in horror. He ran back to Balanchine and Lopokova, waving the paper and crying, *"Serge Pavlovitch est mort!"* —Serge Pavlovitch is dead! (8).

Diaghilev had passed away early that morning in his Venice hotel room. It is a measure of his value to the world of the arts that by that same afternoon, when news traveled without cable television or Internet, Markova read of his death in Littlehampton, 40 miles from where *Dark Red Roses* was being filmed, and Danilova read about it at her hairdresser's in France, 200 miles from Venice.

The man who had called Markova his "new daughter" as he protectively nurtured her career (9)—who had rescued Balanchine and others from starvation in the Soviet Union and taught them principles of artistic production at a world-class level—the man who had united great composers, painters, poets, choreographers, and dancers, who had artistically enlivened Europe through some its most terrible years with vision, grace, and foresight—Serge Pavlovitch Diaghilev was gone.

Dissolve the glue holding a complicated ship together, and the pieces are in for a wild ride across the waves.

Upon Diaghilev's death, his creditors pounced. Sets, costumes, anything worth anything went to pay his many debts. Twenty-five-year-old Balanchine, with 10 Ballets Russes ballets and 32 Monte Carlo opera ballets on his resume, plus a couple of dozen works for smaller places in the off-season, was out of a job. So were Danilova, Lifar, and the rest of the dancers; not to mention the stage manager and all the others involved in Ballets Russes productions.

Jacques Rouché, director of the Paris Opéra, also pounced—on opportunity. The Paris Opéra had long ago lost its reputation for excellent ballet. With Balanchine, Lifar, and other Ballets Russes dancers free to be employed, the Paris Opéra could make a comeback. Would Balanchine stage Beethoven's two-act ballet, *Les Créatures de Prométhée*? In fact, would he become the Opéra's new ballet master?

Balanchine had heard unsavory rumors of the conflicting personalities at the Opéra, but jobs don't grow on grapevines. He ignored a friend's caution that *Créatures* was a bad-luck production and started choreographing it in late October 1929. In two weeks he was so ill with pneumonia that he almost died. The malnutrition he had suffered in Russia and the demanding four-and-a-half years with Diaghilev left his body too run down to combat further infection, and he got pleurisy, a painful infection of the membrane that surrounds the lungs.

Rouché, anxious about his show, agreed to let Lifar take over the choreography. Lifar and a stream of musicians, costume and set designers, and Opéra administrators surged in and out of Balanchine's sickroom, asking advice. The doctor finally banished them all, but not in time to help Balanchine. In an era before antibiotics were available, Balanchine's lungs were now infected with the life-threatening bacterial disease, tuberculosis.

Danilova accompanied him to a sanitarium in the mountains of France, but soon had to return to Paris. The sanitarium physicians recommended surgery on one lung. No, said Balanchine. Losing full use of a knee under the surgeon's knife was enough. Thank you, but he would keep his lungs untouched by surgeon's hands.

After months of pushing high-protein, high-fat food down his tired throat and sitting wrapped in blankets away from direct sunlight, Balanchine recovered. For the rest of his life his left lung functioned poorly and he was subject to spells of weakness, but he was *alive*.

He returned to Paris and the much-relieved Danilova. The two of them bought tickets to see *Créatures* after a brief meeting with Lifar, in which Lifar extolled to them his triumph in the lead role. They enjoyed the show very much. But when they went backstage to congratulate Lifar, the guard at the stage door told them he was not to let Mr. Balanchine or Miss Danilova in—on orders from Monsieur Lifar! Not only that, but a few days later the Opéra announced that Lifar was its new ballet master.

Fiery Danilova announced she would never forgive Lifar. Balanchine, however, immediately put it behind him. He believed, "As a human being, you cannot know in advance what will be best for you" (10), and that something else would turn up specifically for him.

Indeed, now began a series of things turning up. It was winter 1930. Sir Charles B. Cochran hired Balanchine to assemble the *Cochran Revue* in London, on a stage hardly larger than a dining room table. Balanchine created miniature ballets (with Lifar as one of the dancers!). The choreography so impressed visiting *New York Times* dance critic John Martin, he gave the ballets special mention in his reviews. Balanchine considered exploring opportunities in America, but ended up in Copenhagen with the Royal Danish Ballet in August 1930. The RDB directors wanted Balanchine to re-create exact replicas of Ballets Russes pieces. Balanchine, howev-er, modified or even completely rechoreographed as he felt was fitting to the RDB Company and to his own ideas of what should work. This irritated the RDB staff, who thought they had made their instructions clear. By January 1931 Balanchine and the RDB both felt he should leave. He worked again in London for Cochran and for another revue with Sir Oswald Stoll.

The revue pay was excellent. For a brief period, Balanchine lived utterly in the luxurious present. He bought expensive clothes and went horseback riding in stylish Hyde Park. However, he was forgetting Danilova, across the English Channel in France, who was scrimping desperately to keep herself and Dimitriev in her and Balanchine's Paris apartment. Balanchine cabled her at last, saying he was coming back to Paris and was bringing a sporty green car. Danilova splurged on a green outfit to match the car. She greeted Balanchine at the dock, only to find that he could not pay the im-port tax for the car. He gave it away on the spot. Infuriated, Dani-lova opened the boxes of London perfume and lapis lazuli earrings he had bought her, and flung them all at his head.

When Balanchine had to take a short journey on other business, Danilova wrote him that perhaps they should part. She ached for him to reassure her that he wanted her to be his forever, that he would be more thoughtful of their life together, but after a long wait, a letter arrived telling her to do as she thought best.

The Balanchine-Danilova union was over ... but maybe not their working relationship. In the midst of performing as the lead dancer in a musical theater show, Danilova heard that two men named René Blum and Colonel W. de Basil wanted to organize a new company along the lines of Les Ballets Russes. Balanchine, she heard, had been installed as its ballet master. Of course all the former Ballets Russes dancers expected to be rehired, and many were. Danilova had not yet been called. She ran into Balanchine on a Paris street and asked when he would be needing her for rehear-sals. His response was as bitterly unfair as it was shocking: he told the 27-year-old ballerina she would not be needed in this new company because she was *too old.*

While Danilova coped with this humiliation, Balanchine hired three very young ladies, children of Russian émigrés. These girls had studied in Paris with former Imperial Ballet stars Olga Preobrajenska and Matilda Kchessinskaya. Irina Baronova was 12, Tamara Toumanova was 13, and Tatiana Riabouchinska was 14. Like Alicia Markova, their technique rivaled that of many adults. They were physically mature, and looked more like very young women than middle-school students.

The audiences for this new company, Les Ballets Russes de Monte Carlo, dubbed these girls the "baby ballerinas" and met their performances with fervent applause. One ballet featuring Toumanova became especially famous for its tender, brooding story of a lovely ball. It was full of both exuberance and heartbreak, and its title was *Cotillon*. Decades after its choreography was lost to time and Balanchine had made history with other ballets, many looked back on *Cotillon* as his masterpiece.

Once again ballet master for a top-of-the-world company, Balanchine rode high on an artistic wave. But this wave had depths as well as heights. Colonel W. de Basil, peering through little round thick glasses under his lank dark hair, was supposed to be running the business side of the Ballets Russes de Monte Carlo. Unfortunately, he meddled with the artistic side. Balanchine wanted to emphasize Diaghilev's philosophy of breaking artistic frontiers; de Basil wanted to reproduce tradition-encrusted pieces, and dramatize his dancers as Russian exiles yearning for their motherland. De Basil wanted to take money from an American ballerina wannabee and guarantee her starring roles in Balanchine's works; Balanchine responded that his roles were not for sale. The two men clashed repeatedly.

One day Danilova phoned Balanchine and asked why he was giving up the position of ballet master to Léonide Massine, who had just called to hire her for the Ballets Russes de Monte Carlo. It was in this way that Balanchine learned that, as ballet master, he was out and Massine was in! Under Massine, Danilova became the

Ballets Russes prima ballerina, where she would reign for the next 20 years. Balanchine, meanwhile, was once again unemployed.

Perhaps he could have found legal grounds on which to fight to regain his position. Yet perhaps he could also see that if Massine was preferred, then Ballets Russes de Monte Carlo was not the place for him. Léonide Massine was an actor who studied music and dance and had been fostered as a dancer and choreographer by Diaghilev. Massine's grotesquely energetic style centered not on music or movement in themselves, but on stories danced to music, with lavish, frilly costumes and elaborate sets. Balanchine of course used stories, sets, and costumes, but the central language for his ideas was movement itself, directly inspired by music.

Sympathizing with Balanchine were Tamara Toumanova and two other Ballets Russes dancers, Lubov Rostova and Roman Jasinsky. They left Ballets Russes to stick with their young ballet master. Boris Kochno, Diaghilev's librettist, joined this group. Together they pooled their small savings and became their own new ballet company, as penniless as the Evenings of Young Ballet group in Leningrad a decade before, and as enthusiastic. A rich businessman named Edward James heard of their endeavor. He offered them a trade-off: put his wife Tilly Losch into all the leads, and James would pay for theater rentals and other costs. Not in a position financially to argue, Balanchine agreed.

Thus Les Ballets 1933 was born. Edward James's money supplied excellent composers and set designers. Balanchine sweated out seven completely new ballets. His few dancers supported him through long hours of rehearsal. When Les Ballets 1933 opened at the Théâtre des Champs-Élysées in Paris, knowledgeable ballet audiences bought tickets.

Unfortunately, however, Les Ballets Russes de Monte Carlo opened simultaneously at the nearby Théâtre du Chalet. Better financed and staffed with more dancers, its colorful shows attracted big audiences. Balanchine took Les Ballets 1933 to London, only to be followed there and again out-advertised, out-produced, and out-audienced by Ballets Russes.

On the last night of Les Ballets 1933's performing life, Balanchine had to perform in his ballet *Errante* to substitute for the injured Roman Jasinsky. After the performance, Balanchine sat backstage, exhausted, pondering his limited possibilities. A knock sounded at the stage door. Just what he needed—probably someone to tell him about yet another problem.

Instead, Vaslav Nijinsky's wife Romola stood before him. She was in Europe trying to raise money to pay for her husband's health troubles. Beside her stood a tall, awkward-looking young man with close-clipped dark hair and spectacles, wearing an expensive suit. She introduced him as Lincoln Kirstein.

Balanchine's weariness was like cotton in his ears. What came through in Romola's introduction was that Kirstein was a New Yorker with money who for some reason loved ballet. He was writing a biography of Vaslav Nijinsky, which was the reason he knew Romola. He was looking for a ballet master who could establish a ballet company in the United States. Classical ballet, Kirstein was sure, was the medium of choice to inject artistic classicism into the American artistic scene and upgrade American thinking. The ballets he needed would explore specifically American themes. He had the financial backing to employ outstanding artists, composers, designers.

Balanchine's aching muscles competed with Kirstein's words for attention. He agreed to meet with Kirstein three days hence, which would be July 11, 1933. Between now and then he had the depressing task of dealing with Les Ballets 1933's sets, costumes, and financial issues. He saw Romola and Kirstein out the stage door, got himself some food, made it to his hotel room, and tumbled into bed.

What Balanchine did not know about 26-year-old Kirstein was even more than what he had not known about Diaghilev. Like Diaghilev, Kirstein's well-off parents had encouraged their son's interests, which lay in the arts. From his family, Kirstein inherited a sense of responsibility toward the world around him, and a conviction that his family's money should be given to make the world a better place. He therefore invested his time, energy, and money to create avenues for excellent art of all kinds. He both gave money to individual artist friends and supported arts organizations. While earning a degree from Harvard University, Kirstein had started a respected literary journal, *The Hound and the Horn*, and he indirectly helped establish today's Museum of Modern Art.

Kirstein learned that Russian choreographer Mikhail Fokine had a studio in New York City. He took enough Fokine classes to know that he himself would never dance. Yet he felt a deep connection to ballet. He had traveled with his family to Europe and had seen, with admiration, Diaghilev's Ballets Russes perform both *Apollon Musagète* and *Prodigal Son*. On a later trip with a friend to Italy, he stopped to glance into an interesting-looking Venetian church, but had to wait to enter it while a highly decorated black coffin was carried out and loaded onto a gondola. Only after the gondola disappeared down the river, propelled by gondoliers wearing black uniforms with huge red sashes, did Kirstein discover that the body inside the coffin was Diaghilev's.

Kirstein had learned enough about ballet to know that without financial backers, and without impresarios like Diaghilev, ballet as an art form could die out. He believed he had been blessed with money in part to save ballet. He convinced well-connected friends in the United States, especially Edward M. M. Warburg and Everett "Chick" Austin, to donate their resources to help him. Chick Austin, director of the Wadsworth Atheneum Museum in Hartford, Connecticut, had even agreed to allot a large space in his museum for a dance studio.

Kirstein's next step was to interview ballet masters in Europe and see performances to decide whom to ask to come to the United States. He had spoken to Lifar, viewed a Les Ballets 1933 rehearsal and several performances without meeting Balanchine, and decided after seeing Ballets Russes de Monte Carlo several times that he preferred Les Ballets 1933. Therefore he had procured Romola's cooperation to help him meet Balanchine.

On July 11, Balanchine could see from Kirstein's worried eyes that he himself looked, if anything, more exhausted than he had backstage three nights before. Balanchine made himself eat a hearty lunch and hold a spirited conversation about Europe's various ballet companies. The two men listened carefully to each other and scheduled another meeting on July 16. At this meeting, Balanchine decided to come to America and start a ballet company. "But first, a school," he told Kirstein. And he meant a school large enough to endure for decades, feeding a company with fine dancers. Lincoln emphatically agreed. Both men knew that many famous ballet dancers had visited America in the past 100 years, but none had founded a major dance studio or a company.

How much simpler Kirstein's life might have been if Balanchine had just packed his few things and hopped the next liner to New York! No, such matters don't flow along simple channels. Kirstein had to arrange a visa, that is, a document giving Balanchine permission to enter the United States and work. Balanchine, though, wanted Vladimir Dimitriev, who had gotten him out of the Soviet Union, to come along and run the proposed school. This meant two visas, and more money. Oh, and Balanchine wanted 15-year-old Toumanova and her mother to come too . . . *four* visas . . . "We have the future in our hands . . . let us honor it," Kirstein solemnly wrote Chick Austin, and his friend cobbled together the needed travel money (11).

During the rush to prepare for departure, Toumanova was tricked by a deceptive telegram from de Basil into returning to Ballets Russes. Balanchine was not happy with that, but he was even less happy after reaching America, when Chick Austin proudly ushered him and Dimitriev into the studio space in Hartford, Connecticut. Such a small space in such a small American town! What did it matter that wealthy Americans lived in Hartford and the studio was in a prestigious museum? Regarding ballet, these Hartford people seemed to think like amateurs. No, insisted Balanchine, nothing less than New York City and its great stages would do, or he and Dimitriev would return directly to Europe.

Chick Austin had spent hours just arranging for Balanchine and Dimitriev to enter the United States without having to endure the long processing through Ellis Island. Now his generosity in providing a dance space was spurned. Kirstein hastily soothed Austin's understandable outrage and got his Russians back to the city.

From there, the progress toward a studio space went forward while Balanchine's health went backward. During a journey to Philadelphia to interview a ballet teacher there named Dorothie Littlefield, Balanchine's temperature began to rise. Littlefield agreed to join the new school's staff, and Balanchine returned to New York and visited Eddie Warburg's doctor, who warned that Balanchine's tuberculosis might be breaking out in his lungs again.

Kirstein's personality impelled him to frantic outbursts of worry. Here he was trying to cut deals with realtors for a large enough studio in a good enough area to attract clients, and his ballet master might be dying. Balanchine, according to his own personality, reacted with irritating calm. He had brushed near death enough times not to be afraid of it. God was in charge of these things.

Serge Lifar happened to be in New York, as was Misia Sert, in whose mansion Balanchine had auditioned for Diaghilev. Both rushed to Balanchine's bedside with a Russian doctor. Roman Jasinsky and a former Diaghilev dancer named Pierre Vladimiroff also visited. But Balanchine got worse. And he didn't want to enter gloomy Harkness Hospital for treatment.

Kirstein's sister Mina offered to keep Balanchine in her gracious home in Ashland, Massachusetts, so he could get the rest and treatment he needed. With Balanchine settled at Mina's, Kirstein could celebrate, for a few moments, the discovery of a space for their ballet school at 657 Madison Avenue, a block from southeastern Central Park. He could oversee the exacting specifications for a good ballet floor and be there to make the workmen rip out the wrongly installed ballet barres and install them right. He could exuberantly watch the plaque that read "The School of American Ballet" be carefully fastened to the building's front door on December 19, 1933.

Balanchine disciplined himself to rest at Mina's. He recovered enough to be at the School of American Ballet on January 2, 1934, when 22 students took the very first class. With Balanchine, Dorothie Littlefield and Pierre Vladimiroff were the teachers on staff.

An American ballet school headed by an internationally famous ballet master had been created where once there was none. The start-up difficulties were far from over, but the difficult beginning had been accomplished.

Chapter 5
Broadway Detour (1934–1940)

On January 22, 1934, George Balanchine turned 30 years old.

For the first time since age 16, he had no ballet performances to prepare. The hearty American children signing up at the School of American Ballet (SAB) would need years of training to reach performance level. Balanchine was an able teacher, but his fulfillment lay in the complex work of choreography, not in coaching youngsters through their first steps.

The providence on which Balanchine relied apparently saw his distress, for hardly a month later, six male and seven female adult dancers from schools across the United States had joined SAB. A Russian immigrant named Eugenie Ourossow was hired as an administrator and made communication easier between the Russian staff (Balanchine, Dimitriev, and Vladimiroff) and the American staff (Kirstein and Warburg). Ideas began to flow. Enrollment in SAB increased. Soon the adult dancers and older students became the performers in a new company called the American Ballet. All they needed were ballets to perform and a performance venue.

Edward Warburg supplied the initial venue: his parents' extensive property in White Plains, New York, 20 miles north-northwest of SAB. The stage would be small because it would be constructed outdoors on the Warburg lawn, and would have to contain the piano from which the music would come. Balanchine carefully chose ballets he had set in Europe that his American Ballet group could handle: *Dreams*, *Songes*, and *Mozartiana*. He also choreographed two movements of a rich orchestral work by Tchaikovsky called *Serenade for Strings*. He called this new dance *Serenade*. To him it was a tool to teach his less experienced dancers the basics of group alignment, entrances and exits, and unison work. He also showed them how to stay open to interesting ideas. One day a girl rushed in late to rehearsal; another day a dancer slipped and fell. Balanchine used both these incidents to create moments of wordless, deep emotion in *Serenade*.

The White Plains performances on June 9 and 10, 1934, showed the persistence of Balanchine and those surrounding him, for on the first night a downpour in the middle of the show sent audience and dancers running for shelter while the piano was frantically covered up. The second night, a fine drizzle began, but the show went on. In their long floating white dresses, the women in *Serenade* looked entrancing. The 1934 audience of high-society business people did not see the extended version of this work that later became Balanchine's standard. They did, however, see the gracious gestures, the ever-surprising variations of steps that were usually used one way but in Balanchine were used another way, the mind-bending beauty of Balanchine's groupings countered by solo work, and the way the ballet movements followed the music from high-energy to near-rest and back. The damp audience responded with prolonged applause. Seventy-seven years later, arts critic Sid Smith wrote, "In some ways, 'Serenade' has all of Balanchine, all of 20th-century dance, in one gorgeous session" (12).

Back in Manhattan, Balanchine, Kirstein, Warburg, and Dimitriev felt triumphant. But they had to begin a tough process: defining exactly what their company would be. Should it be directly connected with SAB? Or should it be a separate organization that accepted qualified dancers from SAB—and other places as well? How would funds be raised? All four men knew no ballet company ever paid for itself with ticket sales. Kirstein wrote endless letters to potential arts patrons and earned money with lectures about ballet at universities and charitable organizations. Balanchine considered whether accepting invitations to choreograph for theater and opera would drain too much energy from ballet work.

In July, Balanchine had another health scare. On a drive into the country with Kirstein, he suddenly stretched stiff as a board and tried to open the door of the moving car. Kirstein managed to get him to a healing center. Doctors discussed whether tuberculosis had infected Balanchine's nerve centers, but finally Balanchine admitted he had been taking injections of dog hormone to enhance his energy and preserve his youth. The injections were immediately stopped. It would be more than five weeks before Balanchine left the healing center and resumed teaching.

As he recovered strength, he had to consider: Where should his dancers perform next? And, what to perform? What a large team a ballet company needs! Orchestra, set makers, costume makers, advertisers, stage crew, not to mention the choreographer and the dancers. How exacting its requirements are! Large, flat wooden floor, full lighting equipment, dressing rooms, ticket sellers, ushers, printers to make up programs. Also, the right location was critical. Not only should regular citizens find tickets easy to buy and use, but well-off people interested in donating to the arts needed to be invited and be able to access the venue. The performance had to convince these potential patrons that this new company was worth giving their hard-earned dollars.

Balanchine and Kirstein now began a lifetime of plunging into the chilly nothingness of what-shall-we-do-next, and working until they generated that next new thing. To make these performances happen required rare qualities: vision, talent, belief in the value of their work, the ability to unite a team, endless energy, and extreme determination.

Chick Austin arranged performances for December 6, 7, and 8, 1934, at the Avery Memorial Theater in Hartford, Connecticut. Though 100 miles from Manhattan, this theater was in an area populated by arts-conscious people who looked for excellent artists to support. Kirstein wrote the libretto for a ballet that Balanchine choreographed called *Transcendence*. Also programmed were *Mozartiana*, *Serenade*, and an amusing new ballet about high school students, *Alma Mater*.

Their efforts paid off. The Avery Theater shows were seen by such luminaries as producer Sol Hurok, painter Salvador Dali, and actress Katharine Hepburn. These people's approving applause was heartwarming, but their ability to spread the word about this new company was even more important, for word of mouth helped bring in donor dollars and convince more theaters to book shows.

The next choice of venue was far more daring. Edward Warburg and Chick Austin's personal connections had supplied stage space heretofore. Now the American Ballet booked two weeks at the 1,434-seat Adelphi Theatre in central Manhattan. Tamara Geva agreed to come and perform *Errante*, an exotic piece that she danced in an extravagant satin dress. Balanchine also choreographed *Reminiscence*, a showpiece for the dancers' individual capacities, and added *Serenade* and *Alma Mater* to the program.

Opening night, March 1, 1935, started uneasily. The curtain rose an hour late to accommodate latecomers, and the orchestra played *Serenade* so slowly that Balanchine was ready to snatch the baton and conduct it himself. But when the show concluded at 11:30 p.m., he and his weary dancers were rewarded by *22* curtain calls!

The next day, influential critic John Martin gave the show enough good marks to assure ongoing ticket sales for the full two-week run. At the end of the last performance on March 17, a slim figure darted onstage and pumped Balanchine's hand in a congratulatory shake. It was Léonide Massine. This support from a competitor-turned-colleague was yet another boost.

The American Ballet rested during summer 1935, performed in White Plains again in September 1935, and started on a 60-city, three-month tour of surrounding states in mid-October. This tour had been booked by a Russian promoter named Alexander Merovich. Unfortunately, at one of the first stops, he started screaming at the dancers, and within a week was threatening to shoot Balanchine and Kirstein with a pistol. The tour shut down and Balanchine fired Merovich.

Balanchine was quite displeased. Not only had the company lost both its chance to perform and the pay that should have resulted, but a failed tour could so damage the company's reputation that theaters would refuse to book any more shows.

Balanchine did not care about his reputation in itself. His concern was that he had something to say to the world through choreography, and he knew that to say it, he had to build a reputation for fulfilling obligations as well as producing exciting ideas. He had been hoping that the American Ballet might enter into an arrangement with New York City's Metropolitan Opera, similar to Diaghilev's contract with the opera house in Monte Carlo: Balanchine would supply the opera ballets, and then produce full evenings of ballet in the Met's off season. Kirstein had been in contact with Edward Johnson, the Met's general manager. After the Merovich disaster, would Johnson refuse to work with them?

To the relief of both men, Johnson offered the American Ballet a contract. To the frustration of both, the Met proved itself nowhere near so nice a place as Monte Carlo. The Met costume staff refused to clean the stiff, filthy costumes dredged from the opera house basement. The orchestra conductor cut sections of the music without warning Balanchine, so the dancers were thrown into embarrassing confusion in performance. The Met audiences criticized Balanchine's highly original choreography, which disappointed their tradition-bound expectations. When on occasion the choreography was applauded, the singers complained that the dancing was a distraction! Meanwhile, John Martin attacked the Met for contracting with a foreigner instead of promoting homegrown talent. And it looked like the Met would not support a full evening of ballet on its stage for at least a year.

In the face of all this, it is no wonder that Balanchine began accepting opportunities that came from other directions—such as the high-stepping world of Broadway.

For a Russian ballet choreographer to work with tap shoes and jazz music may seem odd. But Balanchine had seen movies with Fred Astaire and Ginger Rogers, and adored them. When the widow of the late Broadway impresario Florenz Ziegfield asked Balanchine to contribute choreography to a revival of the *Ziegfield Follies*, he said yes. Doing so meant a schedule reminiscent of his youthful days racing around Petrograd, choreographing, performing, and studying music: now he hopped subways that bounced him from SAB to the Met to the *Follies* rehearsals. Kirstein shook his head and hoped that the good lung in Balanchine's slender body would hold out.

The Met season, with opera ballets by Balanchine, opened December 16, 1935. The *Ziegfield Follies* opened successfully six weeks later, on January 30, 1936. Also, Chick Austin paid Balanchine to choreograph for the annual Hartford Festival in February (in which Felia Doubrovska gave her last performance). By then Balanchine had already signed a contract to choreograph for *On Your Toes*, music and lyrics by the famous team of Richard Rodgers and Lorenz Hart, set to open April 11, 1936.

Balanchine's work in *On Your Toes* turned Broadway dance in a new direction. At that time, dance numbers in Broadway musicals were pure entertainment stuck at intervals into a story told with music and songs. This same dance-is-decoration attitude had come to characterize ballet in Europe two centuries before. Ballet masters of that era in France, England, Italy, and Austria opposed this low view of ballet. They believed that ballet should accomplish much more than slapdash entertainment and their thoughtful choreography laid the groundwork for the disturbingly beautiful story ballets of the 1800s, such as *Giselle* and *La Sylphide,* as well as Petipa's works.

Now Balanchine applied their principles to Broadway. Each dance number in *On Your Toes* advanced the story instead of suspending the story until the dance was over. The most famous number was *Slaughter on Tenth Avenue*. Tamara Geva was the female lead, and her character was in love with that of Ray Bolger (who three years later became famous as the Scarecrow in *The Wizard of Oz*). Geva's character got gunned down by mobsters during a dance hall piece. A waiter slipped Bolger's character a note warning that as soon as the music ended, he too would die. Bolger's character kept dancing more and more wildly, signaling the band conductor to keep the music going, until the police showed up and saved his life.

Slaughter on Tenth Avenue is now famous as a ballet/tap piece on its own. In 1936, the *On Your Toes* audiences roared their applause. Probably not many noticed that the program credits read *Choreography by George Balanchine* rather than *Dances Staged by*. The word *choreography*, on which Balanchine had insisted, implied a new respect for the role of a dance master in a musical theater production.

Back at the Met, events took an uptick. Balanchine's choreography to music from Johann Strauss's *Die Fledermaus* (The Bat) had pleased Edward Johnson and the Met's board of directors. They offered to let Balanchine have his ballet evening after all. It would open May 11, which didn't give Balanchine much time to prepare, but he was used to working fast.

Unfortunately, he wasn't used to thinking like the Met thought. He wanted to choreograph Christoph Gluck's gorgeous opera *Orfeo ed Euridice*. Not a problem. But he also wanted to hide the prestigious, world-renowned Metropolitan Opera singers in the orchestra pit so the ballet could occupy the whole stage. Huge problem! Only after Warburg agreed to foot the cost for the sets, and Russian set designer Pavel Tchelitchev agreed to get certified with the set designers' union, did the Met board of directors grudgingly agree to hide the singers and let *Orfeo* proceed.

Fighting a nasty cough, Balanchine assembled his dancers. Blond, forceful Lew Christensen, who later founded the San Francisco Ballet, portrayed Orpheus. Lovely Daphne Vane danced Eurydice. Winsome William Dollar was a character called Amor (Love). They and the other dancers were so accustomed to Balanchine that they learned their parts with minimal explanation. Tchelitchev represented the underworld, where Orpheus goes to rescue his wife Eurydice, with eerie graves constructed of gauze pieces, and ladders leaning on nothing. He designed lightweight costumes that covered the dancers decently but left their limbs mostly bare, their muscles rippling as they danced the story of heroic rescue and tragedy.

The opening night audience hated it. Its members knew and loved Gluck's score. Accustomed to realistic sets and costumes, they deemed Tchelitchev's costumes indecent and the set ugly. The next morning the ballet was attacked by New York's critics and by *Time* magazine. Novelist Glenway Wescott defended the ballet in a letter to the *Time* editor, but the Met allowed only one more night of *Orfeo*.

The Met season concluded in mid-June. To Balanchine's surprise, the American Ballet contract with the Met was renewed. Relieved to have the continued income, he looked forward to a restful summer.

Kirstein, unlike Balanchine, had employment rather than rest on his mind for the summer of 1936. True to his mission of developing a truly American ballet company, he booked a 17-show tour of the American Northeast for a temporary company he called Ballet Caravan. He was able to pay the American Ballet's dancers to be in it. Their shows received earnest applause and the tour was extended by another eight dates. Kirstein was pleased. He had gone on the tour, helped with everything from mending tutus to assisting costume changes between ballets—and proved conclusively that American dancers and American-themed choreography could attract audiences.

Balanchine's two-track existence continued during the 1936–1937 season: he choreographed opera ballets for the Met and Broadway dances for a new musical, *Babes in Arms*. Life was stabilizing. Enrollment increased again at SAB, and Dimitriev ran the school competently, though his irritable manner made the other SAB staff dislike him. Broadway paid Balanchine much more money than did ballet, so he used those earnings to help fund his ballet work. Best of all, the Met agreed to let him try another full-evening ballet program, scheduled for April 27 and 28, 1937.

Balanchine decided on an all-Stravinsky program: *Apollon Musagète,* another Diaghilev ballet called *Le Baiser de la Fée* (The Fairy's Kiss), and a new piece, *Jeu de Cartes* (Card Game; its three sections were not called three acts, but "Three Deals"). Stravinsky himself came to conduct. Wearing a fedora hat slouched over his eyebrows and a sly grin, he posed with Balanchine and Eddie Warburg at a table with cards, poker chips, and whisky glasses for the poster that advertised the event.

Balanchine was thrilled. Here he was, the Ballets Russes de Monte Carlo reject, at age 33 creating his own program in America's most famous city, on the stage of its premier opera company, with the composer he revered—it didn't get better than this.

John Martin and other critics politely disagreed. They saw the first performance and praised Balanchine's choreography and the dancing, but, while unanimously declaring Stravinsky a master composer, judged these particular pieces—well—not his best. Undampened, Balanchine and Stravinsky bowed together after the second performance to loud applause, and enjoyed a cast party thrown by wealthy Mrs. Vanderbilt.

As the summer of 1937 approached, Lincoln Kirstein had his own reasons to be excited. Frances Hawkins, manager of the summer 1936 Ballet Caravan tour, had booked no less than 26 *weeks* of Ballet Caravan performances across the United States for the summer and fall of 1937. Kirstein reassembled his company and set off. The troupe enjoyed success: respectable-sized audiences, important critical acclaim, a full page of photos in *Newsweek* . . . but these things occurred without Balanchine and half the 1936 Ballet Caravan cast.

Once again, for Balanchine, showbiz prevailed over ballet biz. Major film producer Samuel Goldwyn had offered him $1,200 a week—an attractive sum in the Depression era! —to choreograph a film response to the *Ziegfield Follies* called *Goldwyn's Follies*. For Balanchine, however, money was secondary to the attraction of a new field in which to learn and experiment. Balanchine had tasted of this new field eight years before in *Dark Red Roses*, the movie he was in the day Diaghilev died. Now, with 25 of his dancers (including William Dollar), he went to Hollywood.

The movie's female lead was a lovely dancer-actress named Vera Zorina. Born Eva Brigitta Hartwig to a German father and Norwegian mother, she grew up eating plain food on a low income while receiving excellent music and dance training. Like Balanchine, Brigitta's early experiences in church (a small Catholic chapel) evoked abiding faith in God: "*He* was my father and He loved me and He would always take care of me" (13). This faith sustained her through a hard yet exciting young life. Her professionally trained parents tried to pursue singing careers, but struggled to keep their marriage going. They separated when Brigitta was 6 years old. When she was 11, her father accidentally drowned. Poorer than before without his support, she performed childish improvised dances in taverns to earn money, which she spent on ballet lessons under Olga Preobrajenska and another Maryinsky exile named Nicholas Legat. Eventually she trained with Anton Dolin. She looked older than she was and danced professionally with Dolin and small European companies from age 13. In 1934, age 17, she joined Les Ballets Russes de Monte Carlo. Colonel de Basil made her pick the Russian name by which she was professionally known for the rest of her career.

Zorina's two years with Ballets Russes were made horrible by Léonide Massine. He seduced her into a sexual affair, promising to divorce his wife. When this divorce did not happen, Zorina left Ballets Russes, broken-hearted and secretly guilt-ridden. Her years with Ballets Russes, however, had given her enough professional renown to make her a candidate for Tamara Geva's role in the London production of *On Your Toes*. She got the part, and fell in love with Balanchine's choreography. She saw Balanchine briefly at a party, chatting amiably with his former wives, Geva and Danilova. When introduced to him, she felt no personal attraction. However, "He was very nice—and that is what I remembered most" (14). Before that brief encounter he was, in her life, a brilliant choreographer. After meeting him, he was also a comforting figure, because he did not leer at her like so many men.

Not much later, Goldwyn offered Zorina a *Follies* contract. She did not sign it until she was certain that Balanchine was the dance master.

Working with Balanchine in *Follies* was choreography heaven for Zorina. He would lead her by the hand to a spot on the floor, stand silently looking at the ground as if listening to something, then start teaching her a movement combination apparently selected from several in his mind—a refreshingly efficient method compared to other choreographers' notes, diagrams, and time-wasting moods. Repeatedly he got dance sequences finished and filmed days ahead of schedule because he could anticipate camera angles and limitations. His dancers were accustomed to the atmosphere of jovial respect that he generated; Zorina was entranced.

An upset provided occasion for Balanchine and Zorina to increase their acquaintance. Balanchine had choreographed George

Gershwin's jazz piece, *An American in Paris*, using multiple camera angles. Goldwyn came to view its progress. Balanchine had Goldwyn and his associates get up periodically and move to different spots so they could see the dance as the movie audience would see it. Annoyed by having to keep shifting position, Goldwyn canceled the entire ballet and walked off the set.

In response, Balanchine disappeared to a Los Angeles resort with Zorina, her mother, and some friends. He and Zorina took long walks, discovering commonalities of faith and European background. His nonjudgmental kindness unlocked the pain she had hidden since leaving Massine. The awful story poured out of her. To Zorina, Balanchine "had something trustworthy and priest-like about him, and I felt that by telling him of my past I would be forgiven" (15). She "became utterly, completely and totally devoted to him. This feeling never changed; no matter how much our lives were altered" (16). Soon after, Goldwyn reconciled with Balanchine and *Goldwyn's Follies* continued production. Balanchine and Zorina worked with a new closeness between them.

Zorina's devotion was not romantic love, but Balanchine did fall in love with her. He waited patiently for her while he made movie history with camera tricks and out-of-the-box choreography ideas in *Goldwyn's Follies*. By the conclusion of filming in October 1937, Zorina had signed to star on Broadway in a Rodgers and Hart musical, *I Married an Angel*—choreography by Balanchine.

Back in New York, while *Angel* rehearsals began, Balanchine also prepared for the Metropolitan Opera season. Clashes kept arising over choreography and how to treat dancers decently. Early in 1938, the Met abruptly canceled its American Ballet contract. Balanchine abandoned his legendary calm and angrily told reporters, "The Met is a heap of ruins, and every night the stagehands put it together and make it look like opera" (17). Kirstein wrote *Blast at Ballet*, an exposé of the Met's misdoings, which evoked so much resentment toward the Met from the artistic world that its management at last begged him to stop.

At this moment in time, Eddie Warburg had to transfer his managing and financial support from the American Ballet to the charitable foundation of his recently deceased father Felix. Warburg transferred the rights to the American Ballet to Balanchine, but without Warburg's funds and a performing home at the Met, the American Ballet ceased to exist.

Balanchine found employment for his dancers in several Broadway shows. When *I Married an Angel* opened in mid-1938, John Martin's column proclaimed, "Balanchine has clinched his right to the title of the first choreographer of Broadway" (18), and Zorina was the toast of the town.

Kirstein, meanwhile, stuck tight to his American ballet vision. He and Frances Hawkins booked a third year of Ballet Caravan shows for summer 1938. Two enduring works that are still being performed, more than 80 years later, resulted from this tour: Lew Christensen's *Filling Station* and Eugene Loring's *Billy the Kid*. For the moment, it appeared to be Kirstein who kept the ballet company dream alive rather than Balanchine.

Balanchine's theater work stayed steady, and so did his desire for Zorina. On Christmas Eve 1938, the two showed up late to a party and informed her mother that they had gotten married before a judge in Staten Island Borough Hall. He was 34; she was 21.

Their union brought them both much happiness at first. Balanchine bought Zorina a house and other costly gifts. She trusted him utterly. As 1939 advanced, they both enjoyed busy Broadway careers and each other.

The year 1940 held downturns for both Balanchine and Kirstein. Unfortunately, the network of roads and theaters across the United States saw ever more groups competing for bookings—not always fairly. Producer Sol Hurok, for example, at that time worked for NBC's National Broadcasting and Concert Bureau. He represented the Ballets Russes de Monte Carlo, which was touring America because it could not return to Europe, where World War II had begun. Hurok, and other businesses such as CBS's Columbia Concerts Corporation, prevented theaters from giving space to smaller competing troupes. Kirstein's dauntless personal energy and funds kept Ballet Caravan, reduced to about 20 doggedly persistent dancers, touring throughout 1939. He offered Balanchine its directorship and an expansion to 40 dancers. But Balanchine, for reasons perhaps never to be fully understood, refused, and Kirstein had to disband the company.

It must have been painful for Kirstein that Caravan dancer-choreographers Eugene Loring and William Dollar immediately found a new company to join. It was called Ballet Theatre. A wealthy dancer, Lucia Chase, started it with manager Richard Pleasant. With Dollar and Loring, they hired the talented British choreographer Anthony Tudor and the American choreographer Agnes de Mille. In its first year of operation Ballet Theatre lost $200,000, but also performed 15 ballets. Eleven of these were new. They depicted psychologically profound, contemporary-themed stories. It is not known whether Balanchine was even invited to participate; but no Balanchine ballets were among that crop. Audiences and critics considered Ballet Theatre's establishment a landmark event, and the company continues strong to this day as American Ballet Theatre.

Meanwhile, several new Broadway shows with Balanchine choreography, not having a music-lyrics team like Rodgers and Hart or a director like Dwight Deere Wiman of *On Your Toes*, turned out to be flops. When a show closes early, its artistic team gets no royalties from ongoing performances. Balanchine's reduced income was a problem because, instead of diligently maintaining his savings account, he had maintained the house for Zorina and her mother, stuffed two pianos into his Manhattan apartment, bought one of the first sporty MG's imported to America, and participated in expensive parties.

He also had invested the last of his savings into a 1940 all-African American musical called *Cabin in the Sky*. Racial segregation, and its bitter oppression of social and work opportunities for nonwhites, was still legal in America at that time. Entertainment was one of the few arenas in which African Americans could make decent money. Balanchine wanted to support African American dancer-choreographer Katherine Dunham and the superb black performers with her, including actor Rex Ingram, opera singer Todd Duncan, and jazz-blues singer Ethel Waters. Producer Albert

Lewis, lyricist John LaTouche, and composer Vernon Duke (Balanchine's friend Vladimir Dukelsky) joined forces with Balanchine. The musical that this energetic team concocted garnered big audiences and high critical praise. But without getting its songs recorded and played on the radio to attract more fans, it could only last so long. A musicians' strike made recording impossible, and the show had to close.

While all this was happening, Zorina began to feel stifled by Balanchine. His way of relating to her did not progress into marital teamship, but remained one of courtship and idealization. As she wrote later, "Women don't want to be idolized, which can be dehumanizing. Women want to be loved for themselves and above all on an equal basis" (19). Understanding this point of view did not come easily to Balanchine. Confused by her own feelings, which included occasional crushes on other men, Zorina separated from Balanchine. She returned when he pleaded with her to do so. Still, their individual careers could not always coordinate, and they saw less of each other.

By now Balanchine had had his fill of musical theater work. More than 20 years later he commented to his first biographer, Bernard Taper, "I'm like a potato. A potato is pretty tough. It can grow anywhere. But even a potato has a soil in which it grows best. My soil is ballet" (20).

Balanchine can hardly be blamed if it looked for a while as though musical theater was where he belonged. But over the years he had seen its prosperous side and its money-losing side. He could honestly compare a life in musical theater to a life making ballets under Diaghilev and with Kirstein. The winner of that comparison was ballet.

Chapter 6
Digging His Own Potato Patch (1940–1948)

In his past, when Balanchine had come to a dead end, he believed, and experienced, that work opportunity would be provided from unpredictable directions. Now was a different time. His savings might be low, but he was not out of work or desperately awaiting opportunity. Instead, he was intentionally choosing what he believed was God's path for him: ballet.

He acted on this belief, not by refusing musical theater work, but by increasing his involvement in ballet. He started teaching more at the School of American Ballet. He found the SAB atmosphere more cheerful because Vladimir Dimitriev had retired. Now Eugenie Ourossow was helped by a new administrator, Natalie Molostwoff. A fine Russian teacher named Anatole Oboukhov had joined the staff. Lincoln Kirstein was general manager. Enrollment was higher than ever. Some students who had started as young children when the school opened six years before had matured to high technical proficiency.

Balanchine had kept many dancers employed in his musical theater choreography. Kirstein, too, found work for dancers, despite having to close Ballet Caravan. Each hour, 12 times a day, 40 dancers performed an 18-minute comic ballet, *A Thousand Times Neigh!* It was choreographed by William Dollar for the Ford Motor Company display at the 1939–1940 New York World's Fair. Not ideal work, but it fed 40 dancers for six months.

The dancers were therefore still in performance trim. Balanchine used as many as he could to set *Serenade* for Massine's Ballet Russe de Monte Carlo. He gave the lead to 20-year-old Marie Jeanne, one of SAB's original students, who had danced with Ballet Caravan. She was a speedy learner and a strong, exciting performer. *Serenade* garnered excellent reviews.

Early in 1941 Balanchine contacted Tamara Toumanova, who was performing in New York. She happily agreed to star in a ballet set to a Stravinsky piece called *Balustrade*, designed by Pavel Tchelitchev. Unfortunately, Tchelitchev's black backdrop behind his bejeweled black costumes obscured the choreography. Critics attacked the ballet. John Martin's column even asked why Russians were again producing in New York instead of Americans!

Vera Zorina was furious with Martin for her husband's sake. Balanchine, however, told her never to respond to a bad review; in fact, if she should run into an upsetting critic, she should say, "Ah, good evening! Nice to see you. Are you in New York?"—as if unaware of the critic's comments. Why let the critic have the satisfaction of seeing your disappointment at inconsiderate, often ignorant writing? (21).

Zorina admired Balanchine's attitude. Nonetheless, she enjoyed satisfaction of her own when she happened to sit by John Martin at a dinner party. She bluntly told him he should not criticize productive artists who were becoming American citizens. Martin, who had never picked on Balanchine's nationality when applauding his Broadway work, had the grace to blush. He later became a strong Balanchine supporter.

Balustrade had not helped Balanchine's effort to reestablish his name in the world of ballet. But World War II generated a fresh opportunity, funneled through Balanchine's most faithful, energetic supporter: Lincoln Kirstein.

In early 1941, the United States had not yet entered the war. Weapons from U.S. factories helped supply the Allies (led by the United Kingdom) against Adolf Hitler's Nazi Germany. In spite of the Allied efforts, fascism was spreading. Fascism opposes democracy and was the government underlying Hitler's Germany. Signs of fascism were appearing in some South American nations. Were these nations to develop ties with Germany, they might become hostile to the United States. The U.S. administration hoped that promoting good relations with these nations would influence them to remain friendly.

Not unlike the Italian city-states of the 15th-century Renaissance, the United States used cultural interchange as one means of diplomacy. Lincoln Kirstein had been active in arts and politics for many years, and had made important connections. His friend Nelson Rockefeller had been appointed Coordinator of Inter-American Affairs by President Franklin Delano Roosevelt. Rockefeller now asked whether Kirstein could assemble a ballet company to tour South America for four months.

Famed French chemist Louis Pasteur once said, "Chance favors the prepared mind." Here was an exciting chance, and Balanchine and Kirstein were prepared. They could honestly represent the United States because, unlike the foreign Ballet Russe de Monte Carlo, their dancers were Americans, trained in America. Also, Balanchine and the Ballet Caravan choreographers had created many ballets, so they had performance-ready pieces. Ten of these were chosen for the tour programs. Balanchine would choreograph four more just for this tour. Kirstein even planned for Balanchine to choreograph pieces while in South America using South American musicians and designers. This collaboration would encourage unity between South Americans and the United States.

Balanchine and Kirstein combined the names of their first two American companies and called their new troupe American Ballet Caravan.

Two months of preparation lay ahead. The dancers underwent inoculations and took pills to ward off diseases like malaria. The dancers under age 22 obtained parental letters of permission to travel and perform. One special blessing in the whole arrangement was paid rehearsal time. The dancers dropped their part-time jobs and devoted themselves to learning ballets.

For his new works, Balanchine chose music he had always loved, and dancers with whom he had worked for years, so once again, choreography proceeded rapidly. Two of the four new ballets became Balanchine classics that remain popular now, 70-plus years later: *Concerto Barocco* (to J. S. Bach's Double Violin Concerto in D minor) and *Ballet Imperial* (to Tchaikovsky's Piano Concerto No. 2 in G Major). Marie-Jeanne led both pieces. She set the standard of feminine speed, strength, and expressiveness that ballerinas ever since have striven to exceed.

Both ballets exemplified a feature of Balanchine's choreography that was unusual for its time: he gave the corps dancers work that was as important to the ballet as what the soloists did. Normally corps members stood positioned onstage adding atmosphere, or danced only in brief spurts, while the lead male and female did the impressive stuff. Not so with Balanchine. In *Concerto Barocco*, for example, the eight corps women danced many interludes while the two lead ballerinas rested. The corps also danced some of the most difficult combinations right along with the leads. Of course the corps enjoyed this. The audiences loved it too, because the active corps works added energy and design, intensifying the ballet's beauty.

Amid long daily rehearsals, three tryout performances of all 14 works at Hunter College on May 27–29, and warnings from Lincoln Kirstein about the difficult conditions of the tour, Balanchine and his company approached departure. They boarded the huge ship *Argentina* on June 6 for a 12-day ride to Rio de Janeiro, Brazil. There they began a week of rehearsals in the Teatro Municipal.

Now the difficulties of which Kirstein warned became real. The box office and stage crews were inadequate, so preparing for the performances took extra time. Some Rio officials criticized the projected program. Two of the dances, Christiansen's *Filling Station* and Dollar's *Jukebox,* were set to music by American composer Virgil Thompson. The style of Thompson's music confused the orchestra members, who missed important cues and confused the dancers.

Balanchine seemed ever more gentle yet strong as he addressed the problems. Kirstein wrote to his parents that Balanchine "has worked marvelously and we really owe him everything. He gets $100 a week and he's worth $1,000. He never complains and is a life saver" (22).

All the trials faded from the dancers' minds when, after seeing *Serenade, Filling Station,* and *Ballet Imperial* on opening night, the Brazilian audience threw fragrant orchids throughout 18 curtain calls! Reviews in next morning's papers were favorable, and at the end of the seven Rio performances, ticket sales almost covered production costs. Not only was this encouraging financially; it also meant that American Ballet Caravan was successfully speaking peace across international boundaries.

The next set of Brazil performances was 250 miles down the coast in São Paulo. Again audiences responded well, though they preferred the more classical pieces such as *Ballet Imperial* to the American-themed pieces like *Billy the Kid.*

Buenos Aires, Argentina, was next . . . or not. The scheduled boat got canceled because, distant though South America was from Europe, the wartime demand for sailing vessels left commercial enterprises with fewer boats. Kirstein finally found a ship that got American Ballet Caravan to Buenos Aires a week late.

Upon arrival the dancers under age 21 had to sit in a freezing prison cell all day while officials examined their letters of permission. Balanchine stayed with them until they were released and delivered to their hotel in the middle of the night. Next afternoon at 2:00 P.M., he had them back in class. At age 14 he had daily walked to the barre in an unheated studio, while hearing gunshots outside and his stomach rumbling inside, and he wasn't going to let his dancers be daunted by a chilly day in jail.

In Buenos Aires and other cities of the region, audience response to American Ballet Caravan varied greatly, as is true of any tour. To Kirstein's delight, Balanchine did choreograph a new ballet called *Fantasia Brasileira,* using music by Brazilian composer Francisco Mingone. South American artists designed and produced the costumes and sets. *Fantasia Brasileira* thus fulfilled a priority goal of the tour.

American Ballet Caravan's next destination was Santiago de Chile, capital of Chile, on South America's west coast. Traveling there from western Argentina presented trouble. The route passed through the intimidating Andes Mountains. A blizzard had just obliterated the roads and train tracks. Kirstein applied his near-magical connecting skills and got 51 dancers, staff, and stage crew onto four small Pan-Air Boeing transport planes. Most of the group had never flown. Imagine rattling in small aircraft between the highest of the spear-like, ice-coated Andes Mountain peaks! The pale-faced travelers clenched their seats until they landed.

Their reward was a 10-day streak of enthusiastic audiences, and—even better—a fully competent orchestra. They left Santiago de Chile energized for the rest of the tour up the South American coast. This last leg had many difficulties, but through it all, Balanchine insisted that others have the better hotel rooms, made sure his dancers received their pay before he did, and was both first to arrive to and last to leave the theater—a true leader by example.

American Ballet Caravan arrived home on November 6, 1941. A month later, on December 7, the American military base in Hawaii's Pearl Harbor was bombed by the Japanese, who had joined the Nazis. President Franklin D. Roosevelt declared war on Japan and Germany. Every able-bodied male was called into military service, including the male dancers and Kirstein.

Balanchine was a U.S. citizen by then, but his history of tuberculosis made him ineligible for enlistment. Therefore, while Kirstein and the others started basic military training, Balanchine started looking for choreography jobs.

By this time his reputation had become international. He set ballets for companies from Argentina to Mexico to Hollywood. He was even asked to choreograph for the elephant act in Ringling Brothers and Barnum & Bailey Circus.

For the circus job, he telephoned Stravinsky:

BALANCHINE: I wonder if you'd like to do a little ballet with me. A polka, perhaps.
STRAVINSKY: For whom?
BALANCHINE: For some elephants.
STRAVINSKY: How old?
BALANCHINE: Very young.
STRAVINSKY *(after long silence)*: All right. If they are very young elephants, I will do it.

Stravinsky produced a piece full of stately dignity, brassy showmanship, and clown-like bounce. Balanchine employed female dancers whose routine included being lifted high on the elephants' trunks. When they fell to the sawdust during rehearsal, Balanchine gently admonished them to land on the balls of their feet, and they climbed right back up. At the end of the initial performances in Madison Square Garden, Balanchine's wife Vera Zorina and Modoc the elephant bowed to each other, heads touching the ground. Then Modoc carried Zorina out of the ring on her trunk, to roars of applause.

Zorina had yearned for Balanchine's return from South America; he wrote letters, but four months' separation was hard. After the circus, he traveled again to Buenos Aires to set more ballets with the Teatro Colón while she signed more film contracts. How glad she was when he returned! They did several projects together. She was thrilled when Ballet Theatre hired her, and she danced in her husband's famous piece, *Apollo*. She was hurt when critics accused her of getting roles on the strength of her movie reputation, not her dance ability. Balanchine defended her in a scathing letter to *Time* magazine.

Shortly after, Zorina wanted to stay with Ballet Theatre instead of finishing a contract to make more movies that she considered meaningless. Instead of understanding her desire to develop as a dancer, Balanchine rather carelessly advised her to finish the contract and get the money. Zorina had never felt so unsupported by him before. The incident marked a downturn in their marriage.

By summer 1944, Zorina and Balanchine no longer lived together. Zorina, age 27, wanted children; Balanchine, she knew, never would. He asked her to accompany him to California, where he was to choreograph an operetta. Frederic Franklin, a Ballet Russe de Monte Carlo principal, was to dance in it. But Zorina refused.

Balanchine hid his disappointment and went to California. He helped Franklin get promoted to ballet master of Ballet Russe de Monte Carlo and solemnly explained, "You know, it's not fun being *maître de ballet*, Freddie. From now on you're going to get up every morning and stand in front of people and give and give and give" (23). To Balanchine, this giving was a commitment for life.

Back in New York, his marriage woes still unresolved, Balanchine donated time to the March of Dimes, which fights polio and other diseases that particularly attack children. In the piece he set, *Resurgence*, he himself portrayed Polio, whose evil hands touched 15-year-old SAB student Tanaquil Le Clerq. The girl fell to the floor and was placed in a wheelchair. As silver coins showered her, representing donations to research, Le Clerq rose from the wheelchair, healed, amid loud applause.

At this time, Balanchine's life seemed more an exercise in "keep on keepin' on" than a life with a defined goal. His marriage was not stable. He was in the right soil (ballet), but still had not found the potato patch where he could truly take root.

His next four years were to be a journey of using his past to create his future.

In very late summer 1944, Balanchine landed an important paying job: resident choreographer with the Ballet Russe de Monte Carlo. This meant steady work with some of the best dancers in America, including his former wife, Alexandra Danilova. He also continued to travel in buses or trains or planes all over the country, doing short-term jobs for smaller ballet troupes. As a result, his name became better known and his choreography influenced American ballet more and more widely. But his work with Ballet Russe was to be especially important, for several reasons.

The first reason was that the Ballet Russe dancers had lost technique (the capacity to do their movements clearly, with precision). Sol Hurok's production schedule was harsh: arrive in a location one afternoon, hurry into makeup and costumes, dance the program, rehearse after the show, gobble a late meal, sleep a few hours, then be packed and on the bus early next morning. Ballet Russe de Monte Carlo brought the grace and beauty of ballet to cities, towns, and villages all over the United States. Its dancers were loved, its return performances popular. But serious practice time was not scheduled in. More and more, when the corps danced its group parts, the choreography looked blurry and boring. The lead dancers' big smiles could not conceal missed turns and lifts.

With ballet master Frederic Franklin's support, Balanchine instituted a daily company technique class. He also arranged for the Ballet Russe dancers to take free classes at SAB whenever they were in New York City. Older dancers appreciated the traditional discipline. Younger dancers enjoyed their increased technical ability. As one dancer commented, "[I]f Balanchine said, 'You can do,' no matter what it was you would try" (24). After some months, critics began to praise the improved technique, especially in the corps.

The next reason Balanchine was important was that his concept of choreography was so different from what audiences expected. Massine and most choreographers used dance to tell a story. Elaborate costumes and sets added much to the visual scene. Music was an underlying addition to the dance, not a prime motivation, the way it was to Balanchine.

By 1945, Balanchine started publishing his own ideas about dance. To him, movement was not a physical representation of sound, or a replacement for words in a story. The movements of dance, in themselves and in their own particular way, expressed the spiritual, emotional, and metaphysical elements of human life. Movement was as necessary to human thinking as sound, words, or visual images in museums.

When Balanchine's first ballet for Ballet Russe premiered on September 10, 1944, it sparked a war of the dance critics that would persist for years. *Danses Concertantes*, to music by Stravinsky, presented dancers in brilliantly colored, compact costumes. The choreography explored the sparkling rhythms and quick turns of mood in the music. John Martin's *New York Times* column derided it as "a clever, somewhat mathematical job of choreography, almost totally devoid of dancing" (25). Poet Edwin Denby's *Herald Tribune* column, however, complimented it, saying its "shift of the figures and of the order of steps is miraculously logical and light" (26).

These opposing views were echoed in many publications. Audiences cheered *Danses Concertantes*, so it stayed in the Ballet Russe repertory. Balanchine did set story ballets such as *Le Bour-*

geois Gentilhomme (The Middle-Class Gentleman). But he also continued setting dances not centered on a story. He called these dances *plotless*. John Martin called them *abstractions*.

All of his ballets had colorful costumes until Ballet Russe did *Concerto Barocco*. Eugène Berman, *Barocco*'s costume designer, disliked the way American Ballet Caravan's costumers executed his designs for the South American tour, so he refused to let Balanchine use the costumes for Ballet Russe. Short on budget and time, Balanchine had the women perform *Barocco* in simple black tunics with pink tights and pointe shoes, while *Barocco's* one male dancer wore black tights, shirt, and shoes.

These stark outfits against a plain light-blue backdrop displeased even Edwin Denby, Balanchine's champion among critics. Writing that he liked *Barocco* but not danced in practice clothes, he would not have predicted that in 10 years, Balanchine's most intensely music-inspired ballets would customarily be performed this way. These ballets made visible the pure partnership of music and movement.

Despite the controversies, by 1946 all critics agreed that Balanchine had raised Ballet Russe's performance standard very high. They also recognized an extremely important cultural transition: from ballet as an exclusively European art to ballet as an American art. World War II prevented Ballet Russe from returning to Europe and hiring more dancers there. When its dancers retired, Americans replaced them. Dancers such as Mary Ellen Moylan, Nicholas Magallanes, Ruthanna Boris, and a spectacular young lady whose father was from the Native American tribe of the Osage, Maria Tallchief, showed that classical ballet could be brilliantly performed by dancers born and trained in the United States.

Tallchief captivated her audiences. She also captivated Balanchine. Late in 1945, Vera Zorina articulated to Balanchine what they both knew: their relationship was no longer that of husband and wife. They remained friends the rest of their long lives, but Zorina wanted to marry Goddard Lieberson, a producer for Columbia Records, and did so after she and Balanchine divorced early in 1946. In August of 1946, 42-year-old Balanchine wed 21-year-old Maria Tallchief.

Why would so young a woman marry a much older man? Why would the man want to spend his days with a woman whose mind and personality were far less developed than his own? Balanchine himself never explained. It seems plain that a dancer who inspired his choreography also stirred his romantic feelings. His humor and his own imaginative romantic ideas were powerful attractions to a lovely young dancer. There in the dance studio, the most important thing in both their lives was happening: she was dancing wonderful choreography and he was seeing his ideas made beautifully real. Perhaps it is understandable that Balanchine seemed to see his relationship with his ballerinas no farther than studio and stage. Motherhood was available to any woman who wanted it, but *ballerina* was a title achieved by the few who dedicated themselves to its demands. He believed he made a ballerina into somebody very special, and he did indeed spur Tallchief to world-class artistry.

At the end of two years with Ballet Russe, Balanchine had succeeded in transforming the company, and in linking his name nationwide more with ballet than musical theater. But the years of constant travel, incompetent orchestras, and variable performing conditions left him yearning for a ballet home and an orchestra whose excellence he could count on. How could he obtain these?

The answer came once more from his most tireless supporter. World War II was over and Lincoln Kirstein was back in New York.

Kirstein and Balanchine's personalities were too different for them to become close friends. Balanchine found comfort and inspiration in his Russian Orthodox faith; Kirstein struggled to define his religious beliefs and suffered bouts of serious depression. Under stress, Balanchine became ever more calm while Kirstein was known for baseless anxiety and abrupt rudeness.

But their commonalities were much stronger than their differences. Balanchine once commented, "Lincoln is a true Christian, even though he won't admit it. He gives you money and runs away before you can thank him" (27). Balanchine himself was generous to friends in need. Both men combined adventurousness with deep beliefs about their life destinies. Balanchine repeatedly walked away from money and security in pursuit of the truest art he could produce. Kirstein often risked every cent of his personal wealth to support the American art he believed in.

Kirstein used his artistic knowledge in World War II. After the war was officially over, but before every location had been secured against Nazi resistance, he risked his life behind enemy lines hunting down priceless art treasures that Nazis had stolen from European museums and castles. Upon returning to New York, he resumed leadership of SAB. While Balanchine was in his last months with Ballet Russe, Kirstein wrote him letters about a new idea called Ballet Society. Whenever Balanchine was in New York, the two men talked the idea over with an orchestra conductor friend, Leon Barzin.

To define this idea, the three men agreed on what they did *not* want: "to tour, or do old works, or take the money that would stop me from working in the way I want to" (28). What they *did* want was complete freedom for Balanchine to create new ballets without worrying about satisfying middle-American commercialized tastes, or restrictions imposed by theater administrators. As Lincoln stated in the written proposal, "We are hungry for an adventurous taste" (29).

If a theater box office controlled ticket sales, then the theater could prevent this "adventurous taste" from reaching full flavor. Most people want to see something they have heard about. Fewer are interested in a complete experiment. Theaters would want ballets that people had heard about and would buy tickets for, leaving only small opportunity for true experimentation. To avoid theater control, Balanchine and Kirstein decided they would just rent the theater space, and sell subscriptions directly to interested patrons instead of selling tickets through a box office.

The first set of performances would take place at the Central High School for Needle Trades. Balanchine had projects in mind for it. During his wealthier Broadway days, he had paid composer

Paul Hindemith to compose a brand-new set of short pieces. Balanchine now choreographed them, calling the ballet *The Four Temperaments*. He also revived a piece he had done for Diaghilev, Maurice Ravel's short opera, *The Spellbound Child*. Meanwhile, he and Stravinsky had begun the process of composing and choreographing a new version of the Orpheus story. Only *Four T's* and *Spellbound Child* were ready for that first program, however.

Many ballet fans in New York City were familiar with Balanchine and Kirstein. The subscriptions sold well. Critics were surprised to find that they would not be given free (complimentary) tickets to encourage them to write reviews, but they were so interested, they bought subscriptions, too. On November 26, 1946, the performance began late; the audience sat half an hour while hammering sounds boomed from behind the closed curtain. But once the curtain rose, in critic Anatole Chujoy's words, the audience was rewarded with "magic on the stage" (30). Those initial performances sparked talk throughout the New York arts world. After the next set of shows, in April 1947, Edwin Denby wrote that Ballet Society might "turn out to have been the origin and foundation of the sensibly organized, exciting American ballet company we need now so badly" (31).

By then, Balanchine was once again dividing his time. Across the Atlantic Ocean, Serge Lifar, still director of the Paris Opéra, went to prison for cooperating with the Nazi occupation of France during the war. In February 1947, Balanchine was offered Lifar's position. He didn't intend to abandon Ballet Society, but its budget allowed it only infrequent performances, and the Paris opportunity was too good to turn down.

With him went Maria Tallchief. He incorporated her into his ballets along with Tamara Toumanova, who had performed so often in Paris that Parisian audiences called her their Black Pearl. Balanchine gave Toumanova a major lead in the first new piece he set on the Paris Opéra Ballet. The music was French composer Georges Bizet's Symphony in C major. Balanchine called the piece *Le Palais de Cristal*. The audiences, and Toumanova, were delighted. They were also thrilled by Tallchief's outstanding speed and musicality. She danced the lead female role of Terpsichore in *Apollo*, among other principal roles.

Balanchine caused some discontent when he cast talented younger dancers in lead roles over senior Paris Opéra favorites. Meanwhile, Lifar's supporters got the accusations against him dropped and demanded his reinstatement as director of the Paris Opéra. By July 1947, Balanchine found himself once again losing his position to Serge Lifar.

Balanchine and Tallchief returned to New York. Kirstein and Balanchine started planning the next Ballet Society program. Dancers long associated with Balanchine as well as teenagers from SAB joined, in spite of Balanchine's long absence, for he and Kirstein created a world into which many wanted to enter. The dancers knew that Ballet Society pay was not good: Balanchine and Kirstein got no pay at all for it, while the dancers earned nothing for rehearsals and only $18.00 per performance. Yet, as ballerina Barbara Walczak later told an interviewer, "The feel of having him set the steps on you—of the music, of the counts, of the kind of kinesthetic movement and quality—was addictive. It felt so wonderful. No other choreographer felt that way" (32). Tallchief commented to the same interviewer that "he brought out the best in each of us. And this is genius. His style allowed a performer's individualism to emerge" (33). For these dancers, better money with Ballet Theatre, Ballet Russe de Monte Carlo, or any other group could not compete with dancing for Balanchine.

The November 1947 performances were not at the Central High School for Needle Trades. Its roomy auditorium was too barren, its stage equipment mediocre. Instead, Tallchief and 17-year-old Tanaquil Le Clerq sparkled through *Symphonie Concertante*, a difficult new ballet, at City Center on West 55th Street. The government of New York City used this hulking former Masonic Temple to house all types of performances at affordable prices. Its stage floor was painfully hard, which can harm dancer's legs, and its wing space was short, so the dancers had to be careful not to run into its wall when they exited the stage. But its lighting and acoustics were excellent, and it was better known and more accessible than the high school.

A sense of momentum combined in everyone's heart with a sense of doom as preparations began for the spring 1948 performances. On the momentum side, Kirstein had obtained the help of a young woman named Betty Cage as general manager. With business manager Frances Hawkins, Cage solved countless logistical problems regarding costumes and administration, freeing Balanchine and Kirstein to focus more on the artistic side. Ballets on two winter 1948 Ballet Society programs sparked rising interest: Marie-Jeanne and Le Clerq dancing *The Triumph of Bacchus and Ariadne* in February, and 38 dancers carrying *Le Palais de Cristal* (renamed *Symphony in C*) in March. The usual division of critical reviews followed *Symphony in C*: John Martin thought it looked tired and over-familiar, while Anatole Chujoy wrote that *Symphony in C* proved that no choreographer alive equaled Balanchine.

With this war of critics once again in the news, ballet fans eagerly followed the progress of the latest Balanchine-Stravinsky collaboration, *Orpheus*. They knew it would be an exciting piece that its world-renowned composer would conduct personally. Ballet Society's move to City Center added to the mounting fascination.

The momentum side was encouraging. On the doom side, Ballet Society's subscriptions barely paid half its costs. Kirstein's personal resources were shrinking. After the spring performances Ballet Society would surely have to fold.

Balanchine maintained his concentration. Whether *Orpheus* would be his last piece for Ballet Society or not, he would do his best with it. He had always been drawn to the Greek mythological figure of Orpheus, son of Calliope, muse of epic poetry. Apollo gave Orpheus his first lyre; with it, Orpheus could make even rocks dance. He daringly entered Hades, the underworld of the dead, to rescue his wife Eurydice when she died of snakebite. With his lyre he charmed Hades' guardians, the Furies, and convinced the gods to let him return Eurydice to the land of the living. The gods agreed on one condition: neither Orpheus nor Eurydice could look backward until after crossing the border between the worlds.

Joyfully the two obeyed until Orpheus's foot stepped into the land of the living. He turned triumphantly to his wife, but she had not quite crossed the border, so he had looked back too soon. Eurydice returned to the underworld. The grieving Orpheus was torn to pieces by Bacchantes, worshipers of the god of pleasure, Bacchus. The Greeks who worshiped him as a divine musician buried his head and preserved his lyre.

Balanchine and Stravinsky thoughtfully developed symbols for the *Orpheus* costumes and set. To represent the command that Orpheus not look back, the dancer who portrayed him would wear a golden blindfolding mask given by an Angel of Death called the Dark Angel. The boundary between the worlds of living and dead would be a giant, billowing white curtain. This curtain would be raised out of sight to show the Furies and the sufferers in Hades when Orpheus arrived, then lowered when he and Eurydice were sent toward the upper world. On their way, Orpheus and Eurydice would dance across the stage in front of this curtain. She would be so overcome by desire for him as to touch him, then wind herself around him. She would slide to the floor where he could not find her. He would grope for her; he would then anxiously remove his mask, only to see her rising to stand beside him. In that instant she would die, fall to the ground, be covered by the outward-billowing curtain, and vanish. Garish, yellow-haired Bacchantes would dismember Orpheus. In the last scene, called the apotheosis, Apollo would visit Orpheus's grave. Orpheus's lyre, garlanded with flowers, would rise from the grave, representing Orpheus's acceptance into divine eternity.

Opening night was in 11 weeks. Three other ballets would be done on the program, which had to be learned. As the weeks sped by, designer Pavel Tchelitchev suddenly left. Isamu Noguchi, designer for modern-dance genius Martha Graham, took on the rushed project of finding materials and executing designs for *Orpheus*.

Only two days before dress rehearsal, Noguchi told Kirstein and Frances Hawkins that the fabric shops would not extend any more credit. He could not obtain the $1,000 piece of China silk needed

for the crucial white curtain. While the three despairingly discussed how to do without it, Balanchine walked in clutching $500
cash in each hand. He tossed it all to Hawkins. Then and forever,
he refused to say where it had come from except that he hadn't
robbed a bank.

Now began the mad days of dress rehearsal. The white curtain
needed rehearsal, too, for human hands billowed it in rhythm with
the choreography. Unknown to Balanchine, a man named Morton
Baum, who had been impressed by a rehearsal of *Symphony in C*,
stood in amazement upon viewing one of the *Orpheus* rehearsals.
Baum left the auditorium, found City Center house manager Ben
Ketcham, and asked who ran this Ballet Society group. Ketcham
told him to find a guy named Lincoln Kirstein.

"Ben," said Baum earnestly, "I am in the presence of greatness"
(34).

Baum was an important member of the City Center board of directors, who wanted a resident ballet company to help build the
city's artistic core. Baum called a fast meeting and presented his
idea: Ballet Society could be that company. Edward Warburg's
brother Gerald warned in blunt language that working with Balanchine and Kirstein was the road to financial ruin. But Baum convinced the board to give Ballet Society a try.

Baum next got Kirstein to his office. He didn't know Kirstein's
personality, so he was surprised when, instead of asking what
Baum wanted, Kirstein unleashed his frustration at the measly so-
cietal support for ballet and the struggle for funds that would end
in disbanding his company after the spring performances. Baum
listened patiently. He then asked if Kirstein would consider turning
Ballet Society into a publicly supported company called the New
York City Ballet.

Articulate, energetic Kirstein sat speechless. Then he was on his
feet, assuring Baum that with that support, in three years New
York City would have the finest ballet company in the world!

In the midst of all this came opening night. The audience applauded the first two ballets, *Renard* and *Elegie*, with Stravinsky
music conducted by Leon Barzin. Then Stravinsky mounted the

conductor's podium, and his wrenchingly pure interweaving of strings with horns and harps enveloped the audience members. They grieved with Orpheus at the grave of Eurydice, stumbled blindly with him into Hades with the Dark Angel, and chilled with horror at the dance of the Furies. They shared his triumph when the gods allowed Eurydice to start back to the upper world, and fell into despair when, in the music's one measure of absolute silence, she died and vanished forever under the implacably billowing curtain. They witnessed Orpheus's grief and helpless destruction amid the wild dance of the Bacchantes, and their spirits rose in sorrowful glory as his lyre rose from his grave to immortality.

The stage curtains shut the lyre from view. The audience sat in silence, overwhelmed. Then someone began to clap, and someone else to shout, and then the audience bellowed and clapped and threw bouquets while the dancers, choreographer, composer-conductor, and musicians bowed again and again. Edwin Denby slumped in his seat, so overcome with emotion that an usher asked if he was okay.

After intermission, the upbeat *Symphonie Concertante* closed the show. But the reviews were all about *Orpheus*. John Martin wrote, "It is an extraordinarily beautiful work, realized in a rare theatrical synthesis" (35). Critic B. H. Haggin called Balanchine "the greatest living creative artist" (36). The City Center ticket office telephones rang off the hook. With satisfaction, Baum scheduled six more performances.

The New York City Ballet was born. It was as if the little lyre on the collar of 9-year-old Georgi had ascended into the 20th-century sky. Or again, it was as if the potato had finally found its soil—indeed, had created its own soil out of persistence, integrity, and talent. Now Balanchine could root and prosper.

Yet Balanchine and Kirstein knew that Baum's offer was not a happy ending. It was a happy beginning. The soil they had found bore rocks, and getting enough rain and sun was still not guaranteed. There was to be much more to the adventure.

Chapter 7
Hard Hoeing: Through Tragedy to Stability (1948–1962)

Yes, the New York City Ballet was born. But for the next six months, it had no performances.

Morton Baum explained what City Center *would* do for its new resident company: starting in late October 1948, the New York City Ballet, or NYCB, could perform on Monday and Tuesday evenings. In addition to providing the performing space, the City Center board would pay some major costs: orchestra, stagehands, advertising, and personnel such as ticket booth agents and ushers. However, City Center would *not* pay dancer salaries, costumes, new music commissions (that is, paying composers to create original music), choreography commissions, or anything else that might arise. On Thursdays through Sundays, NYCB would supply opera ballets.

With the help of Betty Cage, Balanchine wrote letters to ballet fans asking them to donate to cover dancers' salaries. No one responded. While Kirstein hunted down donors to help with leftover Ballet Society debts, Balanchine took a paying job for several months as ballet master to Le Grand Ballet de Marquis de Cuevas. The dancers found whatever work they could until rehearsals began in the fall.

On October 11, 1948, the first-ever New York City Ballet program presented *Orpheus*, *Symphony in C*, and *Concerto Barocco*. Ticket sales were modest, but critics were unanimously satisfied, including *Newsweek* magazine. With opera ballets to bring in cash, the dancers could afford to keep rehearsing.

Momentum gathered around the new company. Two powerhouse dancers from Ballet Theatre signed on with NYCB: Janet Reed and Melissa Hayden. Dancer-choreographer Jerome Robbins, renowned for his Ballet Theatre piece *Fancy Free* and its Broadway offshoot *On the Town*, saw a performance of *Symphony in C*. He loved it so much, he also asked to join NYCB.

Morton Baum then offered NYCB a winter 1949 season of its own: two weeks, six performing days per week, *and* City Center would add rehearsal pay! The budget permitted only one new work for this set of performances—*The Guests*, by Robbins—but ticket sales and reviews were respectable.

And that was all for the next nine months. City Center had scheduled other performing groups and did not need NYCB. Whatever momentum would keep the company going had to come from Balanchine.

He was now 45 years old. The most important tools in his personal survival kit were his hard-earned reputation and his nose for opportunity. His wife Maria Tallchief took a temporary job touring with Ballet Theatre. Balanchine meanwhile set a piece for the latest communications craze: television.

World War II had brought money into the United States through the sale of weaponry. Postwar families had a little more free time and a little more cash than before. Like any new technology, television became a must-have, and a performer was smart who got his face in front of those cameras.

With young Herbert Bliss and Tanaquil Le Clerq in the leads, Balanchine set a television version of *Cinderella*. Many viewers tuned in, but the tiny, rock-hard TV studio floor and the dangerously blinding camera lights made Balanchine leave this new medium alone for several years. *Cinderella* at least supplied some paying work and increased national familiarity with New York City's new home ballet troupe.

When the NYCB dancers reconvened in fall 1949, they had something really new to look forward to: *The Firebird*. Stravinsky had written its music in 1910 for Diaghilev. Smash-hit Imperial ballerina Tamara Karsavina had premiered Fokine's choreography as the mythical Firebird. Thirty-plus years later, Sol Hurok bought its swirly-colored sets and costumes, designed by Marc Chagall, to produce it for Ballet Theatre. When Hurok's relationship with Ballet Theatre ended, he was stuck with storage fees for the sets and costumes. He offered them cheap to Balanchine, who bought them.

Why not? He had the perfect Firebird—Maria Tallchief. She was thrilled.

Redolent of deep-forest mystery, threat, and beauty, Stravinsky's music inspired both dancers and production crew. A remarkable costume mistress named Barbara Karinska redesigned the *Firebird* costumes to replace Chagall's, which had fallen apart. Advertising stirred advance interest among ballet fans.

There was one big glitch in their hopes of good ticket sales: the Sadler's Wells Ballet. This wonderful and very large British company had been founded by Diaghilev dancer Ninette de Valois. During October 1949, while NYCB rehearsed for its November season, Sadler's Wells occupied City Center. Tickets were snapped up night after night for its *Sleeping Beauty*. A hundred dancers, led by star ballerina Margot Fonteyn, leaped and turned amid lavish sets and costumes that were funded by Great Britain's ample royal treasury.

Balanchine and Kirstein sat in the audience, knowing that NYCB was years away from building that level of support for its productions. But they had come too far to give up. Balanchine even talked with David Webster, the general administrator of the Royal Opera House in London's upscale Covent Garden district, where Sadler's Wells usually performed. The two men discussed mounting *Orpheus* there.

Sadler's Wells Ballet then returned to its homeland. Would New York ballet fans have any money left for NYCB tickets? How would NYCB's lower-budget shows compare to *The Sleeping Beauty*?

Two weeks after Sadler's Wells left, Maria Tallchief debuted in *The Firebird*—and spanked the British troupe into the background. Her near-impossible opening solo, with its "many low, fast jumps, near the floor, lots of quick footwork, sudden changes of direction, off-balance turns, turns from point to point, turned-in, turned-out positions one after another" (37), showed her technical power and forceful stage presence as never before. She and her partner, Francisco Moncion, finished their duet to such crashing applause that *Time* magazine compared the audience sounds to "a touchdown roar" (38). One man's trash is another man's treasure, and Hurok's unwanted sets became the opportunity for another stroke of genius by Balanchine.

The momentum continued throughout the fall 1949 and winter 1950 seasons. The variety of new ballets by Balanchine, Robbins, and guest choreographers had the dance and theater world trading comments and buying tickets. Balanchine sensitively calmed 31-year-old Robbins's anxiety about critics' reactions to each new piece. Repeatedly Balanchine told him, "Just keep making ballets . . . and every once in a while one will be a masterpiece" (39).

Balanchine set one of his own masterpieces, *Ballet Imperial*, in March 1950 for Sadler's Wells. With Margot Fonteyn and Michael Somes leading, its Covent Garden premiere earned 17 curtain calls!

David Webster promptly engaged NYCB for a five-week summer Covent Garden season.

Excitedly the dancers and staff boarded a jetliner to England. They all knew this trip was far more than a new performing opportunity. It was a major step on a journey of years that bonded them into a family. Together, they were on their way to boiling point. Water boils at 100 degrees Celsius (212 degrees Fahrenheit). For water to transition from 99 degrees Celsius to boiling point, it must absorb at least as much energy as needed to go from freezing (0 degrees Celsius) to 99 degrees. In the same way, the entire NYCB group—Balanchine, Kirstein, executive manager Betty Cage, dancers, lead stage crew, Madame Karinska's famed costume and wardrobe staff, rehearsal pianists—were united in the transition from local recognition to sustained world acclaim. They sensed that they had not just weeks, but years, of overtime effort ahead, and they were eager to meet the challenge.

Balanchine knew perhaps better than anyone what the challenge would demand of him. His unflagging presence inspired them all. As Barbara Milberg Fisher, one of the dancers, later wrote, "Mr. Balanchine was there with us . . . the teacher who gave company class, the primary choreographer who rehearsed us at home and on tour . . . Sometimes it seemed as if the company were flowing out of his veins" (40).

This bond preserved the troupe's unity through the ups and downs of this first tour in England; and though there were ups, including enthusiastic Covent Garden audiences all five weeks, there were two major downs. One was generated by David Webster, the other by Balanchine.

David Webster was so pleased with the profitable five weeks that he scheduled a sixth Covent Garden week plus four weeks' touring throughout England. Unfortunately, that sixth week was the one in which most Londoners went on vacation, so audiences were very small and the company lost money.

During the free week between the end of the London season and the beginning of the provincial tour, Balanchine waved farewell to Maria Tallchief, who wanted to spend a few days in Paris. Upon her return, she realized that Balanchine and Tanaquil Le Clerq (who was staying with Tallchief and Balanchine in their hotel suite) had developed a romance. Tallchief knew all too personally her husband's history of falling in love with a gifted dancer about age 20. She got her own hotel room. Once again the dancers under Balanchine had to weather a painful readjustment in his personal life.

(Six decades later, much has changed. Greater social awareness of equality between men and women, and of the undue influence older people may exert over younger, make it far less acceptable for a director to forge such close relationships with company dancers than was the case in Balanchine's time.)

The company carried on through four weeks of puzzled orchestras and unenthusiastic audiences outside London. The group returned wearily to the United States and found Morton Baum upset because the extra weeks had changed a mildly profitable tour into a $40,000 deficit. While Baum and his board considered whether they could afford a fall 1950 NYCB season, the company absorbed the difficult shift of relationships among Balanchine, Tallchief, and Le Clerq.

Within the year, Tallchief annulled her marriage to Balanchine based on the fact that she desired children and he did not. Many years after, Balanchine told an interviewer, "I have never left any of my wives. They have all left me" (41). On the surface, that was true. But it is also true that he did not demand of himself the faithfulness on which a lasting marriage rests. Perhaps he was right when he told the same interviewer, "Now I feel I should not have married any of them. The point is, I am a cloud in pants" (42).

Balanchine's marital faithfulness was obviously questionable; but his faithfulness to NYCB was not. Tallchief stayed with the company, and Balanchine continued to give her the lead roles she deserved.

Upon seeing the excellent critical reviews of NYCB's London shows, the City Center board decided to grant a hefty home season of 26 performances from November 11 through December 10. However, there was no budget for new ballets. To help with funds, Baum raised ticket prices slightly and Balanchine agreed to program four repertory-length ballets each night instead of three. (A repertory-length ballet is about 20 minutes long.) Four ballets a night became the standard repertory program from then on.

A scare ripped through the dancers close to performance time because through the grapevine they heard that City Center would not have the funds to mount the season after all. But unexpected profits from an opera, *Meistersinger*, made it possible . . .

And so continued the New York City Ballet. Gifted dancers like Patricia Wilde, Hugh Laing, and Diana Adams signed on. Balanchine inventively managed programs so as to accord with budget restraints, yet maintain variety; Betty Cage later remarked that Balanchine "was wonderful because he always understood the financial limitations" (43). In the winter 1951 season, Ballet Theatre star Nora Kaye and international Russian star André Eglevsky added their talents, while in a mysterious a new ballet called *La Valse*, Le Clerq was elegantly waltzed to death by a man in black. To Morton Baum's amazement, the season earned $150,000 in ticket sales and a small profit!

A year later, after a tour to Chicago and several more City Center seasons, the five-week, 40-performance March 1952 season broke City Center records: $500,000 in ticket sales and audience attendance totaling 200,000. The season did lose $40,000—that's how expensive fully professional productions can be to mount, even if the performers are making no more than decent pay—but Morton Baum and the board were not upset. Their periodic assessment of City Center events showed them that the New York City Ballet was adding prestige to New York City and helping to attract new residents and tourists. City Center support would enthusiastically continue.

This blessing of support granted the company a five-month European tour in spring 1952. The City Center board and others protested angrily because the tour began in Barcelona, Spain, which was under the fascist government of Francisco Franco. Nonetheless, NYCB went.

Its Barcelona season was a smashing success. However, Balanchine had deeper matters on his mind. Kirstein had stayed home to attend to his dying mother. From Barcelona, Balanchine wrote Kirstein that NYCB could not exist just to present new ideas and generate standbys that would guarantee ticket sales. He envisioned reaching out to schoolchildren and to outlying ballet schools that could not afford a trip to City Center. Minds and hearts were enriched through fine art. Souls were strengthened and inspired by wonderful performances. How could NYCB develop an outreach? For Balanchine, hope for the future of New York's citizens and the New York City Ballet lay in using NYCB's gifts for public good.

The European tour continued with overall success through Paris, Italy, Switzerland, the Netherlands, England, Scotland, and Germany. Upon returning to New York, Balanchine wrote a letter to presidential candidate Dwight D. Eisenhower. He told Eisenhower that remembering the needs of the nation's artists in his campaign promises would mean another million votes! Eisenhower did not respond, but Balanchine and Kirstein continued their mission of nourishing their nation's soul and spirit.

In late fall 1952, a group scheduled for City Center canceled, leaving the theater with 6 empty weeks connected to NYCB's scheduled 6 weeks. NYCB took on the whole 12 weeks, longer than any ballet company in the nation had ever run a season, and turned a $30,000 profit! In a spirit of celebration, Balanchine and Le Clerq got married on December 31. The company steamed energetically through 1953 with tours on the American East Coast as well as once again through Europe.

Late in 1953, Balanchine yielded to several years of pressure from the City Center board. They wanted him to produce a story ballet like Sadler's Wells' *Sleeping Beauty*. Forward-thinking, innovative Balanchine had left story ballets behind in Russia. But he couldn't argue that crowd-pleaser works generated ticket sales, and profitable sales generated money for more experimental, soul-nourishing ballets.

Consequently, in February 1954 the City Center curtain rose on a grand holiday party in a big house with a sparkling Christmas tree. Little Marie, the central character, received a handsome doll from her mysterious old Uncle Drosselmeyer. It was a soldier doll, and its jaw could be moved by a handle in the back to crack nuts. Naughty brother Fritz broke the doll, but Uncle Drosselmeyer bound it together again with his handkerchief. As the guests left, Marie fell asleep on the couch, and her mother covered her gently with a shawl. Marie awakened to find the tree growing to a towering height that made the audience gasp (though not as much as those responsible for the production budget had gasped when they found the tree had cost $25,000!). Man-sized mice led by the Mouse King attacked Marie, but Fritz's now-enormous toy soldiers counterattacked. The Nutcracker, full-sized with a whole jaw, appeared from nowhere and dueled the Mouse King, who seemed about to win until Marie flung her shoe at his head and made him stumble. The Nutcracker slew the mouse King. He then turned into a handsome young prince. He took Marie to the Land of Sugar Plums. Snowflakes and candies danced and bowed to the young couple. At last the Prince and Marie left in a sleigh to be together forever.

This colorful scenario included 35 School of American Ballet children as well as most of the 50 NYCB dancers. Forty choirboys from St. Thomas's Episcopal Church somehow crowded onto the City Center stage and sang while Snowflakes in fluffy white tutus leaped and twirled through a swirl of lightweight stage flakes. The Dewdrop Fairy leading the Waltz of the Flowers was Tanaquil Le Clercq, while Maria Tallchief glistened as the Sugar Plum Fairy, with Nicholas Magallanes her handsome Cavalier. Balanchine even had a dancer execute the Candy Cane hoop dance in which he had distinguished himself 32 years before in Russia.

The audience did not know, and did not have to know, that three and a half hours before the curtain rose on Act I, Balanchine was told that the costumes were not yet finished. Balanchine told conductor Hugo Fiorato not to worry because he, Balanchine, had just spoken to Tchaikovsky (who had died 60 years before) and the costumes would arrive on time. Then Balanchine quietly followed the messenger down the street to the costume shop, picked up a costume and a threaded needle, sat down among the frantic seamstresses, and started sewing. Jerome Robbins had accompanied Balanchine. Robbins's impulse to fury about the late costumes was quelled by Balanchine's undisturbed manner. Robbins picked up a needle too. The costumes were sufficiently done by curtain time and the show went on.

Despite the rather surprising reaction of displeasure in John Martin's *New York Times* column next morning—he thought *The Nutcracker* un-Balanchinian, with too much mime and too little dance! —Morton Baum had to add performances to the scheduled winter season because the performances all sold out—and the extra shows sold out as well. Perhaps the picture of Balanchine on the cover of *Time* magazine just before *The Nutcracker* premiered had helped sales; but no, what sold the ballet was Balanchine's assembly of loveliness and charm. Almost 60 years after that first performance, not only by NYCB but by dance companies across America, *The Nutcracker* continues to be performed each Christmas season to large audiences. Balanchine had risen to the bread-and-butter challenge and topped everyone.

The New York City Ballet could now count on regular seasons at City Center, and its budget allowed for more new ballets like *Western Symphony* (even if it did have to be danced in practice clothes the first year, and costumes bought thereafter). Balanchine's visits to Maria Tallchief's Osage family in the late 1940s had gotten him interested in things Western; he loved the tremendous open spaces of the American West, not to be found anywhere in Europe, and even after losing the marriage to Tallchief, he liked wearing Western shirts and string ties, often with a fine vest or a turquoise bracelet.

In 1952 Balanchine had turned down an offer of a $10,000-a-year salary from City Center, so as not to compromise his artistic freedom. He refused even his rightful commissions when he choreographed new works for NYCB. He lived on royalties from performances of his choreography in ballets and musicals. He did his own laundry and ironed his shirts daily before proceeding to the studio for company class and rehearsal. He was more than content with a modest income and the work he loved.

Balanchine's dancers remained as faithful to the company as he. Occasionally, all five of the women he had married—Geva, Danilova, Zorina, Tallchief, and Le Clerq—might be taking his class together. He bore his former wives no ill will. They could separate Balanchine's personal side from his artistic side, and relate to the artistic side. As well, they acknowledged freely Tanaquil Le Clerq's ability to work in any style, her assertive technique, and her brilliant stage presence.

Perhaps greatest of all Le Clerq's qualities was her capacity to participate with Balanchine in the creation of choreography. Powerhouse dancer Jacques d'Amboise, a Queens kid who trained at SAB and joined NYCB in 1949 at age 15, often partnered Le Clerq. Balanchine relied heavily on d'Amboise's capacity for this creative participation, and for decades d'Amboise was a major force in the development of male roles in Balanchine's ballets. Yet even d'Amboise acknowledged that, when it came to reflecting Balanchine's wit and inventiveness in movement, Le Clerq was a master. When NYCB left for another European tour in the summer of 1956, "Tanny," as everyone called her, was one of its ticket-selling attractions.

These European tours were not for the faint of heart. Stages could be hard and splintery. Dressing rooms might be spacious, but were often cramped, dark, and cold. Train rides between cities afforded little real rest. To alleviate the pressure, Balanchine chatted with the dancers on the trains, wrote goofy limericks, and told them which art museums to visit in their slight spare time. It all helped. They toured through Germany and headed through the long dark chill of North European autumn nights toward Copenhagen, Denmark's capital.

Not for 24 years had Balanchine been in Copenhagen. He had not liked the Royal Danish Ballet then, and they hadn't liked him much either. Now he was returning with his own large, internationally recognized company.

The Copenhagen tour started well. The Danish audience in Kongelige Teater applauded the NYCB performances sincerely. But shadows perturbed the company members. They had heard that Stravinsky had suffered a stroke and was expected to live six months at most. Also, they were sensing discontent between 27-year-old Tanny and Balanchine. In their disciplined way, the dancers continued their work as if nothing were wrong.

Then came the worst week of Balanchine's life. Tanny, despite flu-like aches and pains and a strange feeling in her back, had pushed herself through two tough matinee and evening programs. That night, she could not rise from her bed to go the bathroom; Balanchine had to carry her. Several days of special massage therapy made no difference. Pain in her spine and a sudden fever of 106 degrees impelled a mad rush to the hospital, where worried doctors strove to diagnose her illness. Her mother Edith had come on the tour. With Balanchine, she hovered over her daughter. Balanchine also had a fever, but it passed.

At 5:30 A.M. late in that week, dancer Vida Brown heard a knock at her hotel room door. Opening it, she and her roommate Melissa Hayden saw Balanchine standing there white-faced, and heard him gasp, "It's Tanny. She has polio" (44). The two women wept with him until he recovered enough to return to his room.

Balanchine prayed that Tanny could rise again, as she had in the March of Dimes ballet 12 years before. Instead, the doctors advised him of her possible death. Balanchine remained in Copenhagen with Tanny and Edith while the shocked company finished the last two cities of the tour. Ironically, the dancers were offered a polio vaccine during the journey home.

Tanny lived. In March 1957, after five months in Copenhagen with Balanchine and Edith, she could travel back to the United States. For another five months after that, NYCB continued without Balanchine while he tried every therapy he could find for his stricken wife. But Tanny was permanently paralyzed from the waist down.

Settling her in their comfy apartment a few blocks from SAB's new location at Eighty-Third Street and Broadway, Balanchine slowly began again to teach and rehearse. Several times a day he went home from SAB to help Tanny, bringing the groceries, doing the cooking and chores along with Tanny's mother and a maid. He watched cowboy Westerns on television with Tanny, and trained their cat Mourka to leap on cue, comically claiming Mourka owned the body he had always wanted to choreograph for.

Almost a year after that horrifying week in Copenhagen, he began at last to set new ballets—new as in thrusting the ballet universe to a radically different artistic level.

Any new ballet worth watching takes weeks to choreograph. Nobody, but nobody, sets four serious, enduring ballets in four weeks' time.

Until Balanchine.

Building up to the November 1957 and winter 1958 City Center seasons, he produced four pieces whose only common feature was the footwear: pointe shoes for women, ballet shoes for men. Ultra-European *Gounod Symphony* had a male and female leading 20 women in long lightweight tutus and 10 men in handsomely trimmed tunics through traditional ballet combinations. *Stars and*

Stripes displayed regiments of men and women in red-white-and-blue, high-stepping through parade formations to John Philip Sousa's most familiar brass band pieces (arranged by Hershy Kay). *Square Dance* featured famous caller Elisha C. Keeler shouting square dance commands while the dancers flung themselves through impossible ballet combinations—American folk dance through a classical ballet lens. The *Square Dance* music by Arcangelo Corelli and Antonio Vivaldi was 300 years old and was rooted in ancient European folk dance melodies.

The fourth piece utterly broke the ballet history mold. It was quickly set once the dancers were assembled in the studio. Its planning, however, went back three years to 1954; and its significance to NYCB was resurrection, for Tanaquil Le Clerq was not the only one who did not die in Europe. Stravinsky, too, had lived.

In 1954, Lincoln Kirstein had commissioned a new score from Stravinsky. Kirstein wanted to create a trilogy of Balanchine-Stravinsky works, the first two being *Apollo* and *Orpheus*. Stravinsky wrote two-thirds of the new score in 1954, put it aside while touring to conduct orchestral performances of other pieces, then spent late 1956 and eight months of 1957 recovering from his stroke. Despite his impairment, he finished the piece in April 1957. Balanchine at that point was still immersed in Tanny's healing. Once she was comfortably settled, however, he started writing to Stravinsky about this new piece. Stravinsky suggested its cast be eight women and four men; Balanchine agreed. Meeting to work out a plan, the two men fastened long strips of paper together containing the score and scribbled ballet notations. By November 1957, they were ready to take their plan into rehearsal.

For the dancers, the year of grieving Tanny's paralysis had been long. Their empathy for Balanchine during Stravinsky's illness had also been painful. Then came the day when a tiny man with thick glasses and a cane appeared at the top of the steps leading down into the rehearsal studio. He was dapper in his homburg hat, long camel's-hair coat, and gray suede gloves. Stravinsky.

Reverent silence engulfed the room. Then Balanchine and Kolya Kopeikine, NYCB's longtime rehearsal pianist, rushed to help the master composer down the stairs. Balanchine and Stravinsky pored over the score, chattering in Russian and English. Vitality crackled from them like a spreading force field. In that instant, the past was conquered and the future arrived with a holiday bang.

Agon, the new ballet's title, is a Greek word meaning *struggle*; think prot*agon*ist and *agon*y. The ballet's root ideas, though, lay not in conflict, but in musical thoughts Stravinsky had after reading a 17th-century manual of French court dances. Dancers, of course, struggle to define the aim of each movement, discipline muscle and bone to fulfill that aim, then redefine the target at a higher level *and go there*. Nobles of the French court 300 years before also struggled as they danced, not only to learn the steps but to overcome rivalries and divisions. Yet ancient dances and standard ballet forms did not shape, but rather inspired, *Agon*. As Balanchine later described the ballet's initial impetus: "History was only the takeoff point" (45)—a statement that could sum up the life work of both Balanchine and Stravinsky.

Agon's score particularly fascinated Balanchine. To him it carried forward Stravinsky's authoritative grasp of rhythm, and in his later description of the score he commented that even the silence between beats "acts as a carrying agent from the last sound to the next one. Life goes on within each silence. . . . It is all precise, like a machine, but a machine that thinks" (46).

From the dancers' point of view, the 16 short dances organized into five groups were complicated and exhilarating. Balanchine was setting dances for the eight women without the focus on one main ballerina that had been his style until Tanny's illness. As Melissa Hayden, to whom he gave a solo in *Agon*, later remarked, "When he came back, instead of focusing on one woman—which he did with Tanaquil—he started focusing on all the women" (47). Having their gifts more evenly used by Balanchine helped lessen the rivalry between the women that had been keenly present before.

Dancer Barbara Milberg Fisher saw her part in a pas de trois (dance for three) as "all kinds of jumps and fast footwork, abrupt moves and sudden stops, mostly in unison, sometimes sequentially in *canon* mode" (48). Diana Adams performed the pas de deux and commented, "It's not so much the difficulty of the steps or how flexible you are, it's the precariousness" (49)—the sense that she and her partner had to find, every time, the precise edge at which the movements would work. Beyond that edge, balance would be lost and the movement ruined; just short of that edge, the movements would happen, but be dull. Young Edward Villella, only four months a member of NYCB, commented on the "thrill to see [Balanchine and Stravinsky] collaborate. The pleasure they took in the work, their compatibility, not only as Russians and colleagues but as artists, was palpable. We even shared in their laughter. . . . We all felt that *Agon* was a ballet that was going to alter ballet history" (50).

The score made its own music history because it switched in the middle from normative Western harmonic mode to an experimental style called 12-tone. At one point, pianist Kolya Kopeikine cried out, "I'm terribly sorry. There are parts of this music I don't understand." With a reassuring smile, Stravinsky replied, "That's all right. I don't understand them either!" (51).

The music gallops with the catapulting force of a movie chase scene. Dance critic Arlene Croce was later to call *Agon* "wall-to-wall dancing" full of "thrills, danger, apocalyptic energy" (52). When the ballet premiered, all the planning and exploration and joy walloped the audience like a tsunami. Villella described the audience reaction: "I have never, *ever,* heard such screams and shouts of approval in a theater before or after. It was truly unbelievable" (53).

Aptly dollar-minded City Center worked six extra showings of *Agon* into the original schedule.

Yet there was more to *Agon*'s impact even than the music and choreography. The long, powerful pas de deux section was danced by an African American man and a white woman, seven years before the U.S. Congress passed the Civil Rights Act. The woman was long-legged, flexible Diana Adams. The man was 23-year-old Arthur Mitchell, a company member for two years and still ranked in the corps. He was the first African American dancer in America to even become part of a major ballet company, never mind dance a principal role.

Mitchell's presence earlier at SAB and in the NYCB corps had occasioned some trouble. Balanchine in 1955 had paired him for some performances with Tanaquil Le Clerq to replace Jacques d'Amboise, who was then working in the film *Seven Brides for Seven Brothers*. Some parents of corps dancers protested having a Negro man partner a white woman; Balanchine and Kirstein fired their daughters from the corps.

Mitchell knew Kirstein and Balanchine supported him on the basis of his talent, not to condescend to an oppressed group. As Balanchine later told an interviewer, "When I took Arthur there were many objections. . . . Finally, he became integrated, not in a black sense but in a whole sense" (54). Through his ballet company, Balanchine demonstrated that talent has no racial boundaries and that racial prejudice is based on lies.

The success of *Agon* and the other ballets energized the company for their five-month summer 1958 tour to Japan, Australia, and the Philippines. Balanchine decided not to go; it meant too much time away from Tanny, who was still recovering the use of her upper body. Kirstein went only to Japan, as did Tallchief, who wanted to go right back home to her husband, Harry Paschen, with whom she was trying to have a child.

When the rest of the company arrived in Australia, they were met by headlines proclaiming the absence of NYCB's star dancer Maria Tallchief. Result: low ticket sales and poor publicity for the rest of the tour.

Balanchine's response upon his company's return was to eliminate what is called the star system: emphasizing the names of the lead dancers in programs and posters. Subsequent NYCB posters announced upcoming ballets, not dancers' names, while NYCB programs listed the dancers in strict alphabetical order. (Later on the programs changed. The names appeared in three categories designating the rankings that determined the dancers' base pay; highest to lowest, these were principal, soloist, corps. Within each category the dancers' names were listed alphabetically.) Critics such as Olga Maynard in her 1959 book *The American Dance* viewed Balanchine's decision with disdain, or at least questioned his wisdom, but he did not back down. As biographer Bernard Taper wrote, "Balanchine was the first to make the choreography, in effect, the star of the show" (55).

And he kept adding new stars to his choreography constellation. In 1958 he added a pas de deux for Patricia Wilde and André Eglevsky called *Waltz-Scherzo,* and an operetta, *The Seven Deadly Sins*, in which Allegra Kent danced the main character while renowned German singer Lotte Lenya sang the words. In 1959 he set *Native Dancer* for Wilde and d'Amboise, and collaborated with the modern dance genius Martha Graham on *Episodes*. In 1960, while Danish danseur Erik Bruhn was with NYCB, Balanchine set no less than seven ballets, and in 1961, four more, using music ranging from Latin jazz to the clashing noninstrumental sounds of a ballet called *Electronics*, with a noninstrumental score by Remi Gassmann and Oskar Sala. In 1962, Shakespeare got his share of the NYCB spotlight. In *A Midsummer Night's Dream*, Edward Villella soared backward around the stage as King Oberon, Arthur Mitchell bewitched the audience as the magical Puck, and Melissa Hayden ruled as Oberon's queen, Titania. Also that year, Stravinsky and Balanchine collaborated once again on a piece called *Noah and the Flood*, for television.

The dancers who performed these works, in a very literal sense, had to think on their feet. A dancer that Balanchine favored learned roles at top speed and performed them with little coaching. Rather than a drawn-out rehearsal process in which Balanchine verbalized underlying meanings or prescribed precise gestures, he preferred seeing how individual dancers developed their roles in performance. Edward Villella wrote years later, "His credo was, 'Don't talk. Just do.' He'd say it over and over" (56).

In addition to his high production of ballets, Balanchine during the late 1950s laid the foundation for his dream of public service. The company danced for the inauguration of New York Governor Nelson Rockefeller in 1959. In 1960, schoolchildren were brought to City Center for free matinee performances—three thousand children all told—and within a few years small groups of company dancers were being sent by the New York State Council on the Arts to give free lecture-demonstrations in New York City schools and throughout the state.

In 1960 Balanchine also started holding seminars at SAB to which he invited ballet teachers from around the United States. He taught them what he knew about running a school and company. At one gathering he lamented how few outlets for professional ballet existed in so huge a nation as the United States—too few to absorb the talented dancers graduating SAB that he could not fit into NYCB. To foster the efforts of the teachers gathered before him, he promised, "I will help if you want help. I don't have money, but I have costumes, and I have music, and I have some ballets, and I will help you" (57).

Balanchine was as good as his word. He began allowing certain of his ballets to be performed by regional companies (that is, companies composed of unpaid, dedicated dancers, often in their teens). Atlanta Civic Ballet, run by Robert Barnett, who had danced with NYCB in the early 1950s, was the first beneficiary: it staged *Serenade* in 1961. Legally, Balanchine could have charged a pretty penny for the use of his ballets, but he charged not a dime. He traveled to give advice and support whenever he could, even helping a starting company, the Pennsylvania Ballet, find grant money from the newly established Ford Foundation. These helping activities never ceased, to the end of his life.

Lincoln Kirstein meanwhile pursued the dream of arts support in his own way. His personal donations and fundraising for the arts never stopped. He became a member of a board of builders and arts experts who were developing a comprehensive performing center for New York City. As useful as City Center was, everyone recognized that its stage was smaller than ideal for big opera, its stage floor so hard that it posed the danger of impact injuries to dancers' legs, and its wing space much too small for anyone; Marie-Jeanne once exited fast and hit the wall so hard, she was knocked unconscious.

A large area of worn-out tenements in midtown Manhattan was demolished and its tenants relocated to make room for the projected center. At first Kirstein debated whether NYCB should relocate to this center once it was finished, since it had built "the largest, the most faithful, intelligent, and enthusiastic audience in the American theater world" (58) at City Center. But he decided to keep NYCB in the running as the new center's resident ballet company and to insist on making the theater auditorium larger than the original projection of a thousand seats.

To all appearances, the New York City Ballet had entered a period of smooth sailing. It was about to experience a rough ride for the cause of international peace.

Chapter 8
The Farrell Years

The world in 1962 had its eyes on two superpowers: the Union of Soviet Socialist Republics and the United States. Relations between the two were not friendly. Nikita Krushchev was the U.S.S.R. premier (equivalent to a U.S. president). He showed his hostility to the non-Soviet world in 1956 by shouting at Western diplomats in a United Nations meeting, "We will bury you!" Some small nations that were unfriendly toward the United States had aligned themselves with Krushchev, including Cuba, a Caribbean island nation 90 miles south of Florida. Large areas of the world were politically under Soviet rule. Numerous other nations bordering or near the U.S.S.R. had been forced to submit to its power. "Iron Curtain" became the common term for the many miles of fencing and cement guarding the borders of Soviet-possessed countries.

Both the United States and the Soviet Union had nuclear weapons. President Kennedy maintained a terrifyingly delicate diplomatic balance. He asserted U.S. policy against Soviet takeover of democratic nations, while keeping relations with the Soviet Union peaceable.

As a sign of peace, the Bolshoi Ballet of Moscow had performed in the United States in 1959. Balanchine gave the Bolshoi dancers and staff a special showing of NYCB in rehearsal. The Bolshoi dancers hardly understood what they were seeing. They were used to huge obvious preparations for multiple pirouettes, constant repetition of the same major steps from one ballet to the next, and story ballets centered either on Russian legends or Soviet political themes. They didn't know what to think of experimental pieces executed at impossible speed. After the showing, Bolshoi chief choreographer Leonid Lavrovsky elegantly told Balanchine that NYCB would eventually progress to huge story ballets like the

Bolshoi. Balanchine just as elegantly replied that he had left Bol-shoi-type dance 35 years behind him.

In 1961, a world-famous dancer of the Maryinsky ballet, which was renamed the Kirov Ballet in the 1930s, defected to the non-Soviet West. His name was Rudolph Nureyev. His public rejection of his Soviet citizenship heaped acute embarrassment on a nation that was both proud of its ballet and anxious to show its global superiority.

In 1962, a U.S.-Soviet cultural exchange was arranged: the Bolshoi would again tour the United States, and the New York City Ballet would tour the Soviet Union for eight weeks. Stravinsky would undertake a Soviet tour of his own.

Never had Balanchine felt so unenthusiastic about a tour. He had shown the Bolshoi dancers three of his top works (*Serenade*, *Symphony in C*, and *Agon*). Their response ranged from the Bolshoi dancers' puzzlement to Lavrovsky's insults. Would the rest of Soviet Russia respond the same? On top of that, St. Petersburg, now Leningrad, in Balanchine's experience signified starvation, fear, and artistic muzzling. Yet to refuse the tour would make the United States look diplomatically hostile. The company had to go.

The core issue of artistic freedom arose when Soviet officials viewed NYCB's program list before the tour took place. They didn't want *Prodigal Son* (too Christian; official Soviet policy was atheist) or *Agon* (too sexual, they said). Producer Sol Hurok, who had engineered the 1959 Bolshoi tour, entered the negotiations and the ballets were grudgingly approved.

Five weeks of performances in European nations preceded the Soviet tour. A *London Times* reporter who saw NYCB in Zurich, Switzerland, was so impressed that he wrote, "America, and perhaps the western world, is sending what is probably its strongest cultural ambassador" (59) behind the Iron Curtain.

On October 6, the planes loaded with 90 NYCB personnel crossed the dreaded armed border—then landed in Moscow—and Balanchine found himself descending his plane's portable stairway into a crowd of Soviet dignitaries. "Welcome to Russia, home of the classical ballet," intoned one official. Dressed in a silver-embroidered cowboy shirt and pants with cuffs rolled to the ankles, Balanchine retorted, "Thank you, but America is now home of the classical ballet. Russia is home of the old romantic ballet" (60). This reply was not guaranteed to soften Soviet hearts toward Balanchine, but the officials kept quiet and the NYCB dancers and personnel proceeded to their hotels.

Though he presented his normal calm exterior during class and rehearsal in Moscow, Balanchine felt so edgy, he could hardly sleep. His hotel phone would ring at 4:00 A.M. His radio could not be turned completely off. He felt sure the hotel was bugged. The dancers, too, felt uneasy. Doorknobs in their supposedly modern hotel fell off in their hands. A casual chat with a Soviet citizen on the street always ended with the approach of several threatening men in suits. It was nice that Balanchine could reunite with his brother Andrei; Meliton, Maria, and Tamara had all passed away. But even at lunch with Andrei, Balanchine could not relax.

On opening night in Moscow's Bolshoi Theater, audience response to *Serenade* and Robbins' *Interplay* was polite. But politeness changed to warm applause after Diana Adams and Arthur Mitchell's *Agon* pas de deux. There was a sincere ovation after *Western Symphony*. On the second night, Edward Villella's solo in *Donizetti Variations* evoked 20 curtain calls and shouts of "Encore!"—repeat it! To get the program going again, conductor Hugo Fiorato at last violated NYCB policy and signaled an encore, with which the weary Villella complied.

On October 12 the company performed in the Kremlin, Moscow's fortified government center, closing with *Symphony in C.* With unrelenting, joyful applause the audience shrieked, "Bal-an-chine!" until he violated his own personal policy, stepped from his customary position in the downstage right wing, and delivered a gracious bow.

This enthusiastic response continued night after night of the 23-day Moscow tour—even from October 18 to October 28. This period is known to history as the Cuban missile crisis. U.S. aerial photos had revealed Soviet missiles in Cuba, aimed at the United States. President Kennedy now demanded the missiles' removal.

What if Krushchev responded aggressively? Would the dancers become prisoners of war? Balanchine commented solemnly, "I've never been to Siberia"—where Russian political prisoners were sent to be forgotten (61).

Krushchev announced at last that he would remove the missiles. The relief at this news spilled into the final Moscow performance on October 29. After the last ballet, the applause thundered through 20 minutes of curtain calls, at which point Balanchine invited the audience to follow NYCB to Leningrad. As the company boarded the buses to their hotel rooms, ballet fans crowded the curbs, shouting, "Come back, come back, come back!" (62).

Leningrad audiences were equally noisy with enthusiasm, but Balanchine could not feel happy. He visited sites of his childhood memories and discovered his neighborhood church converted into a factory and the Cathedral of Our Lady of Kazan into the Anti-God Museum. His contact with Kirov personnel revealed how profoundly official Soviet policy curbed artistic freedom. He arranged a special NYCB showing for Kirov dancers he had known 38 years before, and for young dancers and musicians. At the reception afterward, Kirov director Konstantin Sergueyev told him, "Thank you. In troubling times which we may share in time to come, try to think of us as we are tonight; we'll try to think of you as you are tonight" (63). With these words he communicated the sense of oppression that was all too familiar to Balanchine.

Balanchine next delivered a choreography workshop, which was well received. Still, he could no longer endure the deep pain and fear haunting him. Thin and exhausted, he flew back to New York City.

The company continued the tour to other Russian cities by train. When they reached the Georgian capital of Tbilisi, 1,800 miles south of St. Petersburg, Balanchine rejoined them. Andrei lived there, and Balanchine at last met his brother's wife and children.

Performances were well received in Georgia. The only drawback was that the hospitable Georgians insisted on holding lengthy parties after every evening's program, so the dancers found adequate sleep hard to come by. With all due appreciation for their hosts and for their part in cultural diplomacy, company and ballet master were quite ready to return to Eighty-Third Street and Broadway for *Nutcracker* rehearsals.

Watchful as Balanchine had been while in the Soviet Union, he had to be watchful in a different way in his and Kirstein's ongoing efforts to develop NYCB. The current matter under watch was Lincoln Center, the performing arts complex being built in mid-town Manhattan. One of its buildings, the New York State Theater, was to house both the New York City Opera and NYCB. At one point, Balanchine decided to view the theater's progress—and none too soon. The orchestra pit was being built for a musical-theater orchestra of about 35 musicians, not the full orchestra ne-cessary for Balanchine's pieces. The stage floor was of concrete, which absorbed none of the shock from dancers' jumps and could cause impact injuries such as lateral fractures of the shinbone. The linoleum covering was not a neutral color, but maroon, which matched the walls of the theater, but would reflect maroon coloring onto the performers when the stage lights shone. The design for theater lighting included poles with stage lights attached, called light trees, that were placed in the wings; these were being in-stalled without considering how the dancers would get past them when entering and exiting.

Getting the wrong sandwich order in a diner isn't a huge prob-lem. Getting the wrong theater as a permanent performing home is. At Balanchine's and Kirstein's insistence, the orchestra pit was doubled to hold 70 instruments. Balanchine and longtime stage manager Ronald Bates together designed a special stage floor of interwoven wood strips, to be covered with gray linoleum. The yield of the wood strips under pressure would preserve dancers' legs from impact injuries. The gray linoleum would not interfere with costume and lighting. And the problem light trees were prop-erly located.

While Lincoln Center was approaching its April 1964 opening, NYCB continued its City Center seasons. For the spring 1963 sea-son, close to performance time, Jacques d'Amboise and Diana

Adams were rehearsing a new Balanchine piece, *Movements for Piano and Orchestra.* Unfortunately, Adams, who was Ronald Bates's wife, had become pregnant and her doctor said she must either have complete rest or lose the baby.

Balanchine's reaction was to cancel the ballet. He often cast lead ballerinas for new pieces without an understudy because his choreography was so much inspired by the ballerinas' individual qualities. Canceling *Movements* created problems, though, because Stravinsky, who wrote it, was already scheduled to come conduct it. Also, getting a substitute ballet going so soon before opening was nearly impossible.

Jacques d'Amboise requested to teach Adams's part to a hardworking, quick-learning 17-year-old corps dancer named Suzanne Farrell. Balanchine unenthusiastically agreed. Farrell hurried with d'Amboise down to Adams's apartment that evening. While Adams lay on her couch and d'Amboise did his best to demonstrate the steps, Farrell struggled to absorb music cues expressed by Adams and d'Amboise as crashes, or booms, or "the sort of pretty music after the messy music" (64). Two days later, Balanchine watched Farrell and d'Amboise rehearse. He was pleased enough to let them continue.

Farrell did her best, but some days further, after a mistakeridden rehearsal, she tearfully told Balanchine that *Movements* was beyond her. He surprised her by saying, "Oh, dear, you let me be the judge," indicating he thought she could do it. Later she found out that Stravinsky, while viewing the rehearsal, had asked Balanchine, "George, who is this girl?" Balanchine replied, "Igor Fyodorovich, this is Suzanne Farrell. Just been born" (65). His words signified how much this dancer had impressed him. *Movements for Piano and Orchestra* went on as scheduled.

An event of immense importance to NYCB occurred at the end of that year, 1963. The Ford Foundation announced it would divide $7,756,000 among ballet companies and schools. What shocked the American dance world was that some of this amount went to five smaller companies, none went to American Ballet Theatre, and the lion's share went to SAB and NYCB. As protests surged and receded, Ford Foundation told Balanchine that for this grant to be delivered, he had to do what he had never done before: he had to accept a yearly salary of $10,000 as director of SAB and $9,000 as director of NYCB, or the deal was off.

Balanchine accepted in his own way. He said yes. Then he hired Betty Cage's helper, Barbara Horgan, to be his secretary, and used his $10,000 as her salary. She was his invaluable personal assistant for the rest of his life.

Now it was early 1964, and NYCB was doing its last season at City Center before moving to Lincoln Center. On the program was *Tarantella*, to Hershy Kay's arrangement of the piece by 19th-century American composer Louis Moreau Gottschalk. It was a magnificently challenging pas de deux for two principal dancers, Edward Villella and Patricia McBride. Villella later wrote that to handle the ballet's speedy direction-changing leaps, he had to re-configure the split-second moments of landing and taking off again. He called the ballet "absolute dance. *Tarantella* is really about the body smiling—it's just one huge grin" (66). At the January 17 premiere, the audience smiled back with loud ovations. No more worries about whether these balletomanes would follow NYCB to Lincoln Center—they were hooked on "wall-to-wall dancing."

The New York State Theater opened in April 1964. It held some wonders: several stories equipped with rehearsal studios, professionally equipped dressing rooms, and a triumphantly large stage with deep wings.

This last wonder, however, presented a problem. The dancers were accustomed to fitting the choreography onto the City Center stage. Now the same movements had to carry them across much more space, "and the whole company suddenly seemed to be out of breath" (67).

Balanchine responded by establishing a much more regular morning company class. A dancer was wise to warm up thoroughly before coming, for Balanchine's classes were not gentle coaching sessions, but were shaped to extend his dancers' skills and address issues that arose in performance. He might work on an outlandish combination in preparation for new choreography. Or he might choose a basic step and demand it be done impossibly slowly. When he felt satisfied with the dancers' form, he would speed the movement up; then speed it again, until the dancers were sure their aching muscles could take no more. But they would try again—and discover themselves able to do the movement faster than they would have imagined possible, in perfect form.

Speed in itself was not Balanchine's goal, but intentional energy. Principal dancer Peter Martins later wrote, "Someone can be speedy and quick and still be dead . . . Whenever you move your arms or your legs, you are saying this is my arm, these are my legs, and I am putting them there" (68). Balanchine used to say, "Don't come on[stage] apologetically" (69). The dancer had to communicate the intention of each movement with an energy that reached the farthest seats of huge auditoriums.

But even intentional energy was not the endpoint of what Balanchine was after. He expressed his ultimate goal to Daniel Duell, who became an NYCB principal during the late 1970s. Duell recalls executing a fiendishly demanding combination of steps in company class. When he finished the combination, Balanchine said to him, "You wish to discover what *I* want and do that. But *I* wish to discover what *you* want" (70). Balanchine, who always disliked being called a genius, seemed convinced that the deep wells of artistic vision within himself existed in others as well. Those deep wells can only be tapped when the artist pushes past his or her apparent limits and discovers, from within, what he or she has to bring to the art form. To this discovery Balanchine called his dancers during his classes—and in performance as well.

By the time Lincoln Center opened, Balanchine had a company of world-class dancers. He also had a superb and stable team of administrators, teachers, choreographers, orchestra conductors, and production crew. His dedicated administrators (Betty Cage, Natalie Molostwoff, Eddie Bigelow, and others), and Kirstein when he was not engrossed in fund raising, provided SAB students and NYCB members empathetic ears. Countless times, they helped solve problems that could never be included in a job description. Barbara Horgan organized Balanchine's packed schedule, starting with her regular phone call to his apartment between 7:00 and 8:00 A.M., when they discussed his day's appointments.

This team surrounded and supported Balanchine the way a football team supports the player with the ball who is running for the goal. A team's support is effective as long as the player's focus does not waver. However, if doubts or faults attack the player from within, the player may falter, and the support team's job becomes harder.

Such a challenge arose from within Balanchine at about the time NYCB moved to Lincoln Center. The challenge centered in young Suzanne Farrell, a truly dedicated artist who gave him, as never before, exactly what he wanted—and drew his fascination in ways that she herself could barely understand. For the next half decade after she performed *Movements*, Balanchine's reality seemed dominated by a fantasy about Farrell that made him deliriously happy, but threatened to erode the New York City Ballet from within. This half decade came to be called "the Farrell years" (71).

Farrell was born Roberta Sue Ficker in Cincinnati, Ohio. During the very late 1950s, the Ford Foundation had granted scholarship money to bring gifted young dancers to major dance centers. Diana Adams had been a Ford Foundation scout and had seen Roberta Sue in a Cincinnati dance studio. Upon receiving a scholarship in 1960, 15-year-old Roberta Sue and her mother moved to New York City. She spent a year or so at SAB, was accepted into NYCB at age 16, and changed her name to Suzanne Farrell. She was not the strongest of technicians; other dancers could turn more times on one foot or jump higher. But she worked with intense dedication, learned roles rapidly, and stood out for her ability to communicate presence and meaning onstage.

She had replaced Adams in *Movements* in April 1963. In December 1963, Balanchine created a new ballet for her and d'Amboise called *Meditation*. Only eight minutes long, the dance depicted a troubled man who is approached by a lovely woman.

She dances comfortingly with him, but then departs and leaves him once more alone.

The theme of a man yearning for an unattainable ideal woman had appeared repeatedly in Balanchine's works. Putting Farrell into a new one of these ballets signified who she was becoming in his mind and heart. His more even treatment of the company women since Le Clerq's illness had not precluded his having favorites like Allegra Kent and Diana Adams, but the attention he started paying Farrell eclipsed everyone else. Before she turned 19 in August 1965, he had cast her in eight major roles.

Reviewers at times commented that Farrell was not as mature as a role needed, but mostly their remarks were favorable. Her talent and dedication were appreciated by other company members. Balanchine's increasing lack of concern for other company dancers was not. Violette Verdy, Melissa Hayden, Allegra Kent, Patricia Wilde, and Maria Tallchief saw roles they had performed for years taken from them and given to Farrell. Patricia Neary, Mimi Paul, Gloria Govrin, and Suki Schorer were among the younger dancers in the company who felt suddenly neglected.

Balanchine gave Farrell a single-pearl necklace and publicly complimented her personal appearance, not just her dancing, in a *Time* magazine interview. These attentions flattered Farrell, but made her uncomfortable. She was a young person who just wanted to dance, and to believe in the leadership of her ballet master. As she herself later commented, "My work, his work, our work, the company's work were the only things worth taking seriously . . . when you believe as I did, you are not yourself anymore; you are your work" (72).

Even though Balanchine's response to Farrell went far overboard, it is not hard to understand why he enjoyed working with her. Like Le Clerq, yet in her own way, Farrell seemed unusually attuned to Balanchine's ideas, and would work with unlimited dedication to make those ideas visible. In rehearsals for a new ballet, *Don Quixote*, Balanchine would present experiments with off-balance turns, backbends, and extensions. "Is it impossible?" Balanchine would ask, and Farrell would respond, "No, it's not. Let me work on it" (73). He could ask anything and she would try it.

In later years Diana Adams remarked to Balanchine that Suzanne adapted tirelessly to any style. He replied, "Well you see, dear, Suzanne never resisted" (74). Perhaps Farrell reflected back to him his deepest visions of adventure and beauty expressed through movement, and also the belief in himself that he craved.

Balanchine did continue creating fine new roles for his other dancers, male and female. The problem wasn't that Balanchine gave the other dancers nothing to do. It was that, as Edward Villella later wrote, "it seemed that Suzanne, and Suzanne alone, had become his reason for being" (75). His near-obsession expressed itself in his May 1965 ballet version of *Don Quixote*, which was based on Miguel de Cervantes Saavedra's 1615 novel. The novel tells of a deluded gentleman who roams the countryside, believing he is fighting giants when he is actually striking at a windmill. He idealizes a peasant woman named Aldonza, and calls her Dulcinea. The book concerns the problem of living unrealistically within an ideal rather than coping with reality.

The premiere of *Don Quixote* on May 28, 1965, featured Balanchine himself in the title role. Farrell appeared and reappeared throughout in several roles: maidservant, damsel in distress, the Virgin Mary, a gypsy, and Dulcinea, the ideal woman. The elaborate production included a windmill, a live horse, and a live donkey.

To critics, Nicholas Nabokov's music for *Don Quixote* seemed unoriginal and the whole ballet disjointed. But what critics commented on most was the relationship of Balanchine to Farrell. She was his new muse, they said, like Geva, Danilova, Zorina, Tallchief, and Le Clerq. Farrell herself did not like the comparison. She knew Balanchine's history of marrying one ballerina, then moving on to another. She had not signed on to be a muse; she just wanted to work.

She did enjoy going to a diner with Balanchine after performances, accompanied by Eddie Bigelow, a former dancer who was now an assistant manager. She realized she could even fall in love with Balanchine, but wanted no involvement because he was still married to Le Clerq, and anyway, he was 42 years her senior. Yet she did not know how to tell Balanchine not to walk her home to her apartment and step in to chat with her mother. She worried whether Tanny would mind.

By late 1965, other ballerinas showed that they minded very much. Patricia Wilde left, as did Maria Tallchief, who stated publicly, "I don't mind being listed alphabetically, but I do mind being treated alphabetically" (76). The company was now without two major ballerinas.

Farrell's developing personhood created further problems. She wanted her own romantic life. She started going out with a ballet fan named Roger. He took her to the current Broadway musical about Don Quixote, *Man of La Mancha*.

Farrell's mother nervously reminded her that Balanchine did not want his ballerinas to date. He was famous for knowing where his ballerinas were and whom they were seeing. He bought them individual brands of perfume, joking that he could locate them by the scent. When after some weeks he saw a small pearl ring surrounded by diamonds on Farrell's finger, he knew it was from Roger. Angrily he demanded Farrell remove it. She did so, and ended her relationship with Roger. Shortly after, Balanchine gave her a larger but very similar ring. She said she couldn't accept it, but he threw it across the room in such a rage that she retrieved it from under the furniture and put it on, shaking. He calmed down.

That this behavior on Balanchine's part was manipulative and unfair was not clear to him or Farrell. In fact, his way of giving his ballerinas wonderful things to dance while dominating their lives was problematic for many of them. He apparently justified it to himself with some confused beliefs that he expressed to an interviewer: that he gave a ballerina a special identity, that she lost that identity once she got married, that once married, her life would conflict with her New York City Ballet life and as a ballerina she would be lost. He said, "It won't do because she must be here *all* of the time, just as I am here *all* of the time" (77).

In the same interview he stated, "You see, man is the servant—a good servant. In ballet, however, woman is first. Everywhere else man is first. But in ballet, it's the woman. All my life I have dedicated my art to her" (78). This idealized man-serves-woman vision was beautifully developed in his ballets, in which the relationship between male and female is never degrading, but ever gracious and gallant, interweaving deep yearning with wholesale happiness. Nonetheless, a harmful self-contradiction lay in Balanchine's claiming that man was servant to woman, while demanding absolute service from his ballerinas.

The ballerinas who remained with NYCB developed individual ways of coping with the whole scenario. They were not yet unhappy enough to dance elsewhere, even if Balanchine did give Farrell the leads in all three of his new works in 1966.

Meanwhile, Balanchine's and Kirstein's alertness to opportunity resulted in the creation of the Saratoga Performing Arts Center, a brand-new open-air summer theater in lovely Saratoga Springs, New York, 175 miles north of New York City. The theater roof covered 5,200 audience seats, with room on the grassy hills for 20,000 more. Starting July 9, 1966, for four weeks every summer, ballet fans from upstate New York and New England could see NYCB without having to travel to the Big Apple, and the dancers had another month of guaranteed work.

The year 1967 brought three new ballets. The most successful was *Jewels*. It had three sections: dreamy "Emeralds" to music by Gabriel Fauré, quirky, jazzy "Rubies" to Stravinsky's *Capriccio for Piano and Orchestra*, and regal "Diamonds" to music of Tchaikovsky. "Diamonds" featured Farrell and d'Amboise. Balanchine had meant "Diamonds" to be the crowning jewel, but it was Edward Villella and Patricia McBride in "Rubies" that drew the most applause.

Another ballet from that year, *Glinkiana*, featured Paul Mejia, a corps member who had been getting cast in soloist roles. Balanchine had noticed him at SAB and appreciated his musicality. He paid for the boy to have piano lessons, and let him use SAB students for a choreography project at his mother's studio in New Jersey.

Another male dancer began a very important relationship with NYCB in the summer of 1967 because he was the only person who could dance Apollo to Suzanne Farrell's Terpsichore. A number of NYCB dancers were taken to perform in Edinburgh, Scotland. Jacques d'Amboise was cast as Apollo, but was sidelined by an injury. *Apollo* was too difficult to teach a local dancer. Another ballet couldn't be substituted because not enough dancers had been available on this trip for such a switch. Assistant ballet master John Taras telephoned all the European companies that had produced *Apollo* and finally got an answer at the Royal Danish Ballet. Twenty-one-year-old Peter Martins had just danced the role in the spring and would come.

Upon arriving in Edinburgh, Martins was thrown into rehearsal, and discovered that the role as he had learned it in Copenhagen did not encompass the out-of-the-box inventiveness of the movements Balanchine had actually created. He did a creditable job in performance, however. After that Balanchine began inviting him to do guest performances in the regular NYCB seasons, often as Farrell's partner.

In October 1967, NYCB performed in Chicago. The *Chicago Sun-Times* set the ballet world abuzz with a piece of inaccurate news: Balanchine and Farrell, claimed the article under a photo of the two, had gotten engaged! Balanchine himself did not deny it. Horrified and embarrassed, Farrell was determined not to allow a scandalous rumor of a love triangle between Balanchine, Tanny, and herself. She told Balanchine that they should no longer eat together after rehearsal and should see each other only in the studio.

During the next several weeks, the NYCB management and dancers could see Balanchine was losing weight and looking sad. Under the urging of those around her, Farrell began to eat with Balanchine again, but she resented their interference in her personal decision.

Balanchine's focus on Farrell continued to evidence itself throughout 1968. She was again the main dancer in his response to the tragic assassination of Reverend Dr. Martin Luther King, Jr., in April. Balanchine created a very moving ballet, set to a 1966 Stravinsky piece called *Requiem Canticles*. White-robed dancers bearing candelabras moved in mournful formation. Farrell, also in white, searched among them for something she could not find, while Arthur Mitchell in purple robes was raised slowly above the stage as if ascending into heaven. *Requiem Canticles* was scheduled only once. It was the closing ballet, after which the audience departed in healing silence.

Balanchine did have other matters on his mind besides Farrell. During 1968, he helped Arthur Mitchell found a classical school and company for minority dancers, called Dance Theater of Harlem. Meanwhile, the administrative burden of running SAB and NYCB increased. The company now had 80 dancers, and SAB's enrollment had tripled since 1958. Public-service lecture-demonstrations continued, and Balanchine's organization continued helping smaller companies, especially by allowing them to produce his ballets as long as they adhered to agreed-upon standards.

Still, his focus on Farrell was plain in other new 1968 works. He revived *Slaughter on Tenth Avenue* and cast her in Geva's role. *Metastaseis and Pithoprakta* also featured her. By the end of 1968, ballerina Patricia Neary announced she had had enough of the favoritism for Farrell, and departed.

Balanchine hardly had the inward resource to react to the loss of yet another important dancer, for he was by now all too aware that a romance had developed between Farrell and Paul Mejia. One night the 64-year-old ballet master shocked Farrell by not only asking her to marry him, but by offering to have children with her. Farrell later wrote, "It broke my heart not to be able to give him everything he wanted, but I couldn't. I couldn't and survive at the same time. This was something I could not explain; I just felt it" (79).

To accept her refusal was too difficult for Balanchine. On February 5, 1969, he flew to Mexico and obtained papers for a legal divorce from Tanny. Then he went to fulfill a choreography commitment in Germany. He was not in New York on February 21 to see Farrell and Mejia quietly married. But they knew that he found out, for he did not return as scheduled. Barbara Horgan, Lincoln Kirstein, and Eddie Bigelow all ended up in Europe, reasoning with him while he swore never to return. At last he did come back, but outside of rehearsal he hardly spoke to Farrell at all. At one point she found him in his office and offered to leave. He muttered that Mejia should leave instead. Mejia's name appeared less and less frequently on the casting sheet, an unmistakable sign of Balanchine's disfavor.

One person, who knew Balanchine perhaps better than anyone, saw how the situation would develop and did something to help out: Tanny Le Clerq. Before flying down to Mexico for the divorce papers, Balanchine had called her and tearfully informed her of his decision to divorce her. "Nice," she responded wryly. She had probably seen it coming. As soon as she hung up with Balanchine, she called Jerome Robbins and asked him to return to NYCB (80).

Unpopular though Robbins was at times for his irritability during rehearsals, the dancers could think of no one better qualified to help the company through the Farrell crisis. He agreed to come, and started setting a pas de deux for Villella and McBride that expanded into *Dances at a Gathering*: five couples romping to piano music by Frédéric Chopin. This wonderful piece was set to premier on May 8, 1969. Villella was also scheduled to dance *Symphony in C* that night, but asked to be released because *Dances* was so draining. Mejia had just danced the *Symphony in C* role and was the only logical choice to replace Villella, but when the casting sheet went up the morning of May 8, Mejia's name wasn't on it.

Farrell was so upset that she sent Balanchine a message saying that if Mejia did not dance that night, both he and she would leave. When she arrived at the theater in the evening, her weeping costume mistress informed her she was no longer scheduled to dance. This could only mean she and Paul had been fired. Wide-eyed with shock, the couple left, ultimately finding work in Europe.

Dulcinea was gone.

Balanchine produced only one more ballet in 1969: *Valse Fantasie*. Nobody liked it.

Deflated Balanchine was; but not dead. There was life beyond the fantasy he had centered on Suzanne Farrell. One excellent change was SAB's move to a handsome new facility in The Juilliard School, which was part of the Lincoln Center complex. Another good thing was the return of Patricia Neary, who danced the Siren in *Prodigal Son* and then, at Balanchine's request, flew to Europe to become ballet mistress of the Grand Théâtre de Genève in Switzerland, which Balanchine had helped establish.

Meanwhile, lovely ballerinas such as Kay Mazzo began to take over Farrell's roles. Another ballerina, Karin von Aroldingen, had developed a sweet, sustaining friendship with Balanchine after he gave her fatherly advice during a 1969 tour. She too assumed some Farrell roles. During 1970 Balanchine created two ballets with von Aroldingen as one of the leads: jazzy *Who Cares?* to music of George Gershwin, and flowing, emotional *Suite No. 3* to Tchaikovsky's piece of the same title.

The critics approved. They also applauded the outstanding male dancers who joined NYCB permanently in 1970: Peter Martins, Helgi Tomasson, and Jean-Pierre Bonnefous. All three remained stalwart assets until their retirement from performing many years later.

The critics unfortunately did not applaud Balanchine's joint effort with Arthur Mitchell in May 1971. The two men decided to mount a benefit performance to fund-raise for Dance Theater of Harlem. (Tanny Le Clerq was part of the whole effort, for she was a DTH dance coach.) In an effort to use their dancers according to their strengths, Balanchine and Mitchell had NYCB dancers perform the more abstract sections of a piece called *Concerto for Jazz Band and Orchestra*, while the DTH dancers carried the jazz, mambo, and boogie-woogie parts. The critics attacked Balanchine for obvious white-black stereotyping. He abandoned his ice-cold reaction style and shot back, "If people were offended by the benefit, let *them* sponsor a benefit, and let *them* do what they want. . . .

They will only talk. I don't talk. I *do*" (81). He pointed out that too many African American children were steered early away from ballet instead of being allowed to develop the way Mitchell had. He continued his public support for Mitchell's effort. Forty years later, Dance Theater of Harlem remains an important American ballet institution.

Works for NYCB by Balanchine and other choreographers in this period were stirring little enthusiasm, except *In the Night, Goldberg Variations,* and *Watermill*, all by Robbins. By early 1972, critics generally viewed Balanchine as a ballet master in decline. Perhaps it was understandable; he had lost Farrell, and on April 6, 1971, he also lost Stravinsky, who died after a lengthy illness just before turning 89. What inspiration did Balanchine have to continue? Was the momentum gone altogether?

The rumor mongers were in for a spectacular surprise.

Chapter 9
Ballet Genius of the Century (1971–1980)

Rosemary Dunleavy was an NYCB dancer who later became a teacher and rehearsal leader for Balanchine. She once remarked that if Balanchine told her about an idea, within a year he would make it happen.

Premier dancer Jacques d'Amboise, in his autobiography, relates how Balanchine would describe to him entire scenarios of ballets such as *Medidation* or *A Midsummer Night's Dream* as long as a year before scheduling their first rehearsals.

During NYCB performances, Balanchine customarily stood in the downstage right wing, watching. On June 17, 1971, Barbara Horgan was beside him. He turned to her and said, "Next year, Stravinsky," then returned his gaze to the flowing movement onstage. She knew better than to ask what he meant. He would let everyone know when the time came (82).

While the rumor mongers whispered of his low prospects, he started conferring with Stravinsky's wife Vera and friend Robert Craft. After consulting with several prominent European arts personnel, he approached Richard Clurman, chairman of the New York City Ballet Board of Directors. This group of dedicated professional men and women helped raise money and make critical decisions about NYCB's finances. The board had made possible NYCB's 35 performing weeks in the 1971–1972 season, more performing than the Bolshoi Ballet or the Royal Ballet of London. The board also helped establish the regular cycle of performing seasons, which enabled ballet fans to buy regular season tickets, making a regular budget possible.

As Mr. Clurman listened to Balanchine's grand idea, he must have liked the sound of it. Balanchine proposed a week-long festival of all-Stravinsky ballets. It would open June 18, 1972, which would have been Stravinsky's 90th birthday

But listening further must have made Clurman's heart pound. Balanchine envisioned performing 36 ballets on the seven programs, of which 26 would be brand-new—all to be prepared in nine months! Why, the most ballets Balanchine had produced in a year was 7 (not counting opera ballets), yet he intended to set 11 of the new Stravinsky ballets himself.

Even more staggering, he insisted that, for the entire week prior to the festival, the New York State Theater must close for rehearsals instead of remaining open for regular season performances. To Clurman, this proposal must have sounded like Balanchine was drilling a dark hole in the NYCB budget. However, Balanchine showed Clurman carefully worked-out figures and asserted that the large audiences that would attend the festival would make up for the money lost during the rehearsal week.

The board decided to support the festival. Balanchine whetted the appetite of the ballet world with a press conference at a favorite Manhattan restaurant, the Russian Tea Room. Madame Stravinsky came. So did Vera Zorina's husband, Goddard Lieberson, because he was chairman of Columbia Records, which produced all of Stravinsky's recordings. To the journalists crowding in, Balanchine raised a glass of vodka, proposing a toast to Stravinsky, who, he said, had been a genius like Einstein. He explained that the first night of the festival would display ballets to Stravinsky's earliest works, culminating with his latest works on the final night. Seven choreographers would set the 26 new ballets, one of whom would be Léonide Massine's son Lorca. "We will show Stravinsky's life through sound and then you will see the whole thing in front of you," he rejoiced (83). Repeat performances were projected to run in Munich and Paris.

Conductor Robert Irving, aided by Robert Craft, started extra rehearsals for the NYCB orchestra in mid-May. Choreography of the new ballets started much earlier. As spring advanced, Diaghilev himself could never have imagined the pandemonium. More than 80 dancers scurried from studio to studio, learning new ballets and relearning old ones at hurricane speed. In one studio, Edward Villella slouched with his nose close to the ground as the Italian comedy character Pulcinella, while Violette Verdy as his spunky girlfriend twinkled behind him on her toes. In another, Karin von Aroldingen looped her extraordinarily flexible body through impossible shapes. A few doors down the hall, Kay Mazzo and Peter Martins explored tender gestures with hands and head that would be dramatically emphasized by spotlight while violins sighed sweetly. In yet another studio, Patricia McBride scampered elegantly with Helgi Tomasson through a story ballet pas de deux.

Nondancers were part of the crowd, too. Journalists came in and out, as did Betty Cage, Lincoln Kirstein, Barbara Horgan, and friends of the choreographers. The dancers chatted, laughed, sweated. Jerome Robbins preferred absolute quiet in the studio when he was choreographing, and once asked Balanchine how he could concentrate amid the "chattering, knitting, coffee-drinking crowds of people" (84). Balanchine replied that when he was a youth, harsh taskmasters maintained rigorous silence among the dancers during rehearsals, and he never wanted his dancers to endure that sense of oppression.

Meanwhile, the regular spring season began in early May, which meant that a dancer might rehearse starting at 10:00 A.M. both for the festival and for the current season, then rush into makeup and costume and perform in several ballets; or dance the first ballet of the evening and then gallop back upstairs for another two-hour Stravinsky rehearsal.

A festival souvenir booklet was produced to sell at intermission. Madame Karinska and her team cut new cloth, refurbished old seams, and invented different costumes using leftovers of past ballets. Ronald Bates and his stage crew practically lived at the theater during the last rehearsal week, setting lights that would suit the many moods of the pieces and complement the costume colors. Leslie "Duckie" Copeland, supervisor of the men's wardrobe, later remarked, "You really didn't mind coming in at eight o'clock in the morning and working until eleven at night if need be because it was for the family. . . . And Balanchine was always fun to be around" (85).

An observing journalist asked what Balanchine would do to relax after all this hard work. Balanchine grinned, "It's not hard work, and I don't relax—why should anyone want to relax?" (86). He was doing what he was born to do.

The festival opened and the crowds came. They saw not 26, but a still-magnificent 21 new ballets, 8 by Balanchine and a 9th, *Pulcinella*, a collaboration between Balanchine and Robbins. On closing night, as the last notes of the somber, meditative *Symphony of Psalms* faded, the audience received small glasses of vodka. Balanchine and Kirstein onstage with the dancers led a joyful toast to Igor Stravinsky.

The NYCB board must have been happy that 86 percent of the festival's costs were covered by ticket sales alone. And they must have been happy with reviews of the festival. The critics called Balanchine the Shakespeare of the dance world, the genius ballet choreographer of the century. Three of his new works were unanimously hailed as masterpieces: *Duo Concertant, Stravinsky Violin Concerto*, and *Symphony in Three Movements*.

But he hadn't done the festival in order to be hailed as a genius. "Above all else," Suzanne Farrell later wrote, "he wanted the audience to hear the music, really hear it, and if his dances enhanced that experience, he considered his job well done" (87). Balanchine himself commented that if the Stravinsky Festival ballets bored his viewers, they could just "close their eyes and hear a marvelous concert—of music nobody else is playing" (88). For him, the festival had never been a gamble. It was all win-win.

Compared to the festival, the four-week summer season in Saratoga Springs seemed relaxing. After Saratoga, an important tour got added into the company's 1972 schedule: four weeks in Russia.

For Balanchine, this trip was not loaded with the personal pain he had experienced in 1962. It was, however, important for its revelation of how effective Balanchine training was in producing superbly capable dancers, right down to the newest corps member. Since 1962, Russians had become much more knowledgeable about Balanchine; but the Kirov dancers and teachers who now watched him give class in Leningrad were quite surprised that he did not train his corps dancers separately from the soloists and principals. In Russia the corps and soloists had no expectation of attempting principal-level class work. Not only did Balanchine's whole company take class together, but the corps members could keep up with the principals in the most difficult steps. Once again, by raising the bar of excellence for his own group, Balanchine had raised it for the dance world.

Back in New York after the tour, life at NYCB was pleasantly stable. Balanchine's apartment on Sixty-Seventh Street was a five-minute walk from the New York State Theater. On a typical day he rose early, breakfasted lightly, spoke with Barbara Horgan, ironed his shirt, and did other minor chores. Then he went to the theater, where he attended to the matters Barbara Horgan had apprised him of in their early-morning conversation.

At 11:10 A.M., he walked into the studio where he held company class. "A-a-*and*," he would say, and send his dancers through a rapid series of grand plies (slow deep-knee bends designed to safely build strength), ports de bras (bends in different directions with standardized arm positions), and battements (pointing the legs and feet at low, medium, and high levels) (89). In his teaching, as in his choreography, he knew exactly what he wanted, but was always open to useful revelation from a dancer. For example, when he was trying to express how a dancer should end a jump noiselessly by controlling the landing of the heel, corps dancer Daniel Duell suggested a verb: *to resist.* Balanchine was delighted and used *resist* often thereafter.

The level at which Balanchine's school and company had stabilized stood in marked contrast to the Ballet Society days of 1946. During the 1971–1972 season, NYCB gave 230 performances for more than 500,000 people. Graduates of SAB found jobs with every major company in North America and Europe (except the Royal Ballet, which hired British subjects only). Any ballet company could have a Balanchine ballet free upon agreeing to learn it from a Balanchine-approved regisseur, to give Balanchine proper credit, and to perform it without changes. Many companies took advantage of this fine offer. Royalties from these ballets could have fattened Balanchine's bank account. However, he still refused to charge because he knew most companies could never afford to pay.

In 1973, Balanchine mostly programmed dances done during or before the Stravinsky Festival. But he did choreograph one new dance: *Cortége Hongrois*. Its purpose was to celebrate the retirement of Melissa Hayden. She had joined NYCB in 1949. She was so beloved a performer that from the mid-1960s NYCB audiences regularly applauded her upon her first appearance in a program. Now age 50 and looking at least 15 years younger, she led a large group through glittering classical combinations with her longtime stage partner, Jacques d'Amboise, while Karin von Aroldingen and Jean-Pierre Bonnefous led their contingent stomping through the Hungarian *czárdás* folk dance. *Cortége Hongrois* became an enduring piece of NYCB repertory.

By now Balanchine was 69 years old. He had choreographed a bag of masterpieces. Though he always preferred to think of the future rather than preserving the past, he knew he should record his company's ballets. Several favorites, like *Cotillon* for Les Ballets 1933 and a late 1950s piece, *The Figure in the Carpet*, had disappeared forever because neither Balanchine nor his dancers could remember the choreography. So he arranged to film NYCB repertory at a television studio in Berlin during September.

Edward Villella had done TV work many times. He warned of the 12-hour days and the cramped, hard floors. Balanchine waited patiently while the dancers decided whether to go, voting through their union: the American Guild of Musicians and Artists (AGMA). Balanchine himself had encouraged the development of artists' unions in the 1940s, for he had experienced the unsafe conditions endured in the past by too many nonunion dancers. With his support, his dancers exercised their voice in the decisions that impacted them.

To his satisfaction, 81 of the 83 company dancers chose to accompany him to Berlin. At Balanchine's stern insistence, the filming took place not in tiny, cement-floored TV studios, but in huge rooms with wood floors, and the lengthy days were made easier by mandated union rest breaks. "Everything union does is minimum," he was known to say. "For me, I don't want minimum for my dancers. I want maximum" (90). Years later, Balanchine expressed fierce regret over the whole Berlin effort, because the camera crews were more interested in fancy angles and trick shots than in straightforwardly recording the choreography. Nonetheless, the archive was of immense historical importance to the dance world.

The company returned from Germany to discover that the New York City Ballet orchestra was threatening to strike. Balanchine couldn't believe it. Weren't the musicians being paid according to contract? Yes, responded conductor Hugo Fiorato, but why should city garbage men get paid more than highly skilled, experienced musicians? "Because garbage stinks!" responded Balanchine (91). Some of the dancers even queried whether they, too, shouldn't be paid more than garbage men; Betty Cage quietly pointed out that if money were the issue, the dancers could apply for employment with the city's sanitation department. Nothing Balanchine or anyone else said could prevent the musicians' strike, and the NYCB season opened a month late after a bargain was struck and the musicians' salaries raised.

During this period, Balanchine commented on his beliefs to his biographer, Bernard Taper. Regular Bible reading had assumed great importance to him. He had always been convinced that God had created him to get people dancing in ballets. When his time on earth ended, God would take him to heaven, like Stravinsky and Tchaikovsky. These beliefs carried him through the stresses that arose during his journey of obedience to God's purpose. Perhaps it is understandable that many people, like NYCB Chairman of Education Nancy LaSalle, felt that Balanchine gave them a "spiritual center" (92).

Balanchine never let himself become too heavenly minded for earthly good. His mission was both to educate and to entertain. His difficult ballets forced his audiences to think in new directions; his entertaining ones reminded them of life's beauty and joy.

His first new ballet of 1974 would have to be classified as difficult. Balanchine set it to a score that composer Pierre Henry didn't even call music, but a "sonority" (93). Its title was *Variations pour une porte et un soupir* (Variations for a Door and a Sigh). John Clifford, wearing grayish-white, crept onto a darkened stage while human sighs swirled from the loudspeakers. Brightening lights revealed Karin von Aroldingen, her hair shaped in a black pixie cut, her facial features erotically exaggerated, and her upper body clad in white, with a vast black skirt covering the entire stage. She remained in one place, bending her flexible body to bitter creaks of a door. For 20 minutes of sheer concentration, apart from all musical or movement tradition, she and Clifford interacted with the sighs and creaks until first Clifford, then von Aroldingen, disappeared into the mammoth black folds of the skirt and the curtain fell.

Perhaps some in the audience understood Balanchine's attempt to show "man's weakness—how he strives to get involved but, once there, doesn't know how to get out" (94). The viewers either liked it or absolutely hated it. Enough education, their overall attitude said.

Six months later, aided by Alexandra Danilova, Balanchine took his audiences back to 19th-century France in his premiere of *Coppélia.* To Léo Delibes' lush, cheerful orchestral score, Patricia McBride danced the lead role of Swanilda in the fairy tale of an old toymaker trying to magically invest life into human-sized dolls. Helgi Tomasson danced Swanilda's young fiancé, Franz. Balanchine cast large groups of children in all of the village scenes (thus filling the auditorium seats with delighted parents). Unanimous applause from audiences in both Saratoga and New York City showed they didn't consider this ballet difficult at all.

Soon after the 1974 Saratoga season, Balanchine received a surprising two-line note from Suzanne Farrell. She and Paul Mejia had watched one of the Saratoga performances. She requested to return to NYCB: "Is this impossible? Love, Suzi" (95).

Five years had passed since Farrell's departure. She and Balanchine had both grown personally. He sent no romantic notes, but through Barbara Horgan invited Farrell to his office, where he greeted her with a friendly hug and a glass of wine. They worked out a contract. Without fanfare, she appeared for company class in late December. Then-soloist Frank Ohman remembered that moment: "Mr. B. rolled up his sleeves and he hugged her and she got back to work" (96). She returned to performing for the winter 1975 season in her old role in second movement *Symphony in C.*

Initially Kay Mazzo, and others who had hurriedly filled in for Farrell five years before to keep programs uninterrupted, felt uncomfortable and anxious about her return. But Balanchine's obsession did not rekindle. Farrell's roles were shared and she was cast in few roles that had not been created on her. The only sign of the hurt Balanchine had undergone five years before was that he did not offer Paul Mejia a contract. Mejia found directing and choreography work elsewhere, and became co-artistic director of Maria Tallchief's Chicago City Ballet. He and Farrell ran summer workshops near Saratoga during the company's annual Saratoga residency. Farrell guested often with Chicago City Ballet and helped Mejia program Balanchine works there.

Farrell did continue to inspire Balanchine with her high ability to perceive and make visible his artistic ideas. Though ballet was Balanchine's soil, his experimentation with music and motion reached far beyond ballet's forms. During 1975 he mounted another festival, this time centered on French composer Maurice Ravel (1875–1937). Both of the Balanchine works that endured from this festival departed far from classical format. One, *Le Tombeau de Couperin*, fascinated the eye the way ocean waves do, or flames: eight couples in two quadrilles (geometrically arranged groups) danced apart, together, in canon, in imitation, in opposition.

The other dance, *Tzigane* (Gypsy) began as a solo for Farrell. To a lone violin whose sound reflected the random beauty of life in a wilderness, Suzanne Farrell reached, plunged, twisted, and swirled, her many-ribboned black-and-red skirt and soft light-colored blouse seeming windblown. Without the support of one classical step she managed to embody the violin's unpredictable sound, until at last she was joined by Peter Martins and four couples in a final romp.

Following the Ravel festival, Edward Villella nervously approached Balanchine. Villella, a native of Queens, had been of foundational importance to NYCB since he joined it in 1957. His masculine dancing had helped American ballet retain the balance between male and female. His artistry had evoked many of Balanchine's most outstanding roles for men. Villella had also furthered the education of Americans toward excellent dance via frequent guest appearances with other companies and on television.

However, being a man, Villella's experience of Balanchine differed from that of women. During the late 1950s and early 1960s, though Villella was trusted with starring roles, he and at times the other company men encountered Balanchine's critical, insulting side. Another issue concerned Balanchine's company class. Villella's SAB training had been interrupted when he had to go to college. He determinedly did ballet exercises during those four years. When he returned to SAB, he was taken into the company and put into rehearsals. The gaps in his training were not addressed. His taut musculature afforded him explosive power and speed, but the demanding movement exploration in Balanchine's class left him with agonizing cramps. By 1962 Villella discovered that he was greatly helped by taking class with a Danish teacher, Stanley Williams (who became SAB's foremost teacher for men until his death in 1997). From the mid-1960s Villella took daily class only with Williams. Balanchine thus lost the chance to explore Villella's capacities in company class, and Villella wondered whether Balanchine ever quite forgave him.

Now Villella told Balanchine unfortunate news: his hip had lost the cartilage that protects the leg bone from grinding directly against the pelvic bone when the leg moves in the hip socket. This condition was so painful that Villella had to proceed very carefully just to get out of bed each day. His career as a premier dancer was over.

As Balanchine listened, he shook his head in disbelief. He surprised Villella by compassionately touching his arm and assuring him that NYCB would try to help. For several years Balanchine and Robbins found ways to use Villella's magnetic stage presence without making technical demands he could not meet. Eventually Villella founded his own outstanding company, the Miami City Ballet.

Balanchine made 1976 start well with two new works. *Chaconne*, to the music he loved from Gluck's *Orfeo*, featured Peter Martins and Suzanne Farrell, backed by fine soloists and company members. Four months later audiences shouted and laughed for *Union Jack*, a magnificent and witty tribute to Great Britain. *Union Jack* had an immense cast of 70-plus dancers, historically authentic costumes of the British Isles, and authentic traditional Scottish and Irish folk dances. It was a companion piece to the 1958 *Stars and Stripes*.

Then, in a sort of dreary déjà vu, the NYCB orchestra struck again for higher pay—in the middle of *Nutcracker* season, when it would hurt ticket sales worst. Balanchine's response was an icy statement that he had started from scratch before and would do it again, orchestra or no—brave words from a man of age 72. He wasn't bluffing, but fortunately negotiations with the NYCB board finally bore fruit. Near the end of winter season 1977, the orchestra once again filed into the New York State Theater pit. The audience usually applauded the orchestra's appearance. This time, they booed.

Balanchine wasn't about to let the atmosphere surrounding his company go sour. He soon had company and orchestra busy preparing *Vienna Waltzes*, which premiered June 23, 1977. Lead couples Karin von Aroldingen with Sean Lavery, Patricia McBride with Helgi Tomasson, Sara Leland with Bart Cook, Kay Mazzo with Peter Martins, and Suzanne Farrell with guest dancer Jorge Donn led a large cast through the history of the waltz. Rouben Ter-Arutunian, a longtime set designer for NYCB and other fine companies, created remarkable scenery. It began in a forest glen, then transformed in sequence to a brassy dance hall and a sparkling high-society café. The final scene was a ballroom, whose high-mirrored backdrop magnified the elegance of the women's swirling white dresses and the men's tuxedos. The audience response was to buy out the succeeding performances and gobble up *Vienna Waltzes* souvenir booklets.

The 1977 projects weren't over yet. Balanchine pounced on an opportunity afforded by producers Merrill Brockway and Emile Ardolino to add to the film archives created in 1973. Brockway and Ardolino rebuilt the vast stage floor of the Grand Ole Opry House in Nashville especially for dance. Starting in 1977, they broadcast six programs of Balanchine works for *Dance in America*, which reached millions of television viewers. Also in 1977, a new edition of *Balanchine's Complete Stories of the Great Ballets* reached bookstores. Its 800 pages described 372 ballets from around the world and throughout ballet history, with supplemental material such as a glossary—a must-have for any serious dancer.

On January 19, 1978, a short work premiered by a new choreographer: Peter Martins. *Calcium Light Nite*'s stage setting was the exact opposite of tradition: side curtains and backdrop raised to expose the backstage ropes, pulleys, and stored equipment, with light provided from a huge square of neon light tubes hung over the stage. (Neon lights, or calcium lights, use calcium in the chemical reaction that provides illumination.) The quirky, upbeat music was by American composer Charles Ives. New York City Ballet then-soloists Daniel Duell and Heather Watts bounded through individual variations and a pas de deux that ended with both kneeling, hands pushing each other's heads unexpectedly away, startling the audience into laughing applause. Martins' double career as choreographer and principal dancer had begun.

Balanchine premiered two works of his own that same month. *Ballo della Regina,* to an ultra-classical orchestral score by Italian composer Guiseppe Verdi, had Merrill Ashley and Robert Weiss flashing through purely classical variations at unmatchable speed. *Kammermusik No. 2* was quite different. Composer Paul Hindemith had set a piano rollicking through orchestral instruments like a rollercoaster on the hunt. Colleen Neary, partnered by Adam Lüders, and Karin von Aroldingen with Sean Lavery, led eight men (no women!) through stark geometric movements with superhuman energy.

None too soon were these things accomplished. Balanchine had been strangely tired lately, and worse, mildly dizzy. On March 15 he felt so miserable that Barbara Horgan and Eddie Bigelow drove him to his heart doctor. Diagnosis: mild heart attack!

After two weeks of observation and testing in New York University Hospital, and most of April 1978 resting at home, Balanchine felt better. He had things to do. One was to return the calls of Mikhail Baryshnikov, a superb Kirov dancer who had defected from the Soviet Union three years before. Over dinner, Balanchine agreed to take him into NYCB.

Baryshnikov knew he would receive no star treatment. He gave up a per-show fee of $3,000–$5,000 with American Ballet Theatre to make $750 weekly as an NYCB principal. To those who found his decision financially foolish, he commented, "My Russian friends will understand at once and rejoice. There [the U.S.S.R.] Balanchine is an incredible symbol of uncompromised creative genius" (97). Baryshnikov was soon engaged in NYCB's customary crush of learning roles as fast as he could think.

Baryshnikov's arrival coincided with the premier of a ballet called *Tricolore*, a tribute to France. Balanchine intended it as a companion piece to *Stars and Stripes* and *Union Jack*, but his heart attack made him too ill to finish it, so he assigned its sections to Robbins, Martins, and principal dancer Jean-Pierre Bonnefous. Balanchine was well enough to attend its premiere. He tried to be encouraging, but everyone could see that *Tricolore* didn't work.

For the first time, the unthinkable question hovered and descended: How would NYCB manage if Balanchine's health failed?

In accord with his nature and his trust in God, Balanchine did not *re*act with what-if talk, but *acted*. He called a lawyer, started the process of making a will, and went back to rehearsal.

He then acted on something else important to him. He took Suzanne Farrell to supper. She was puzzled when he opened a Bible, recited the Lord's Prayer in Latin, then focused on the part of the prayer that says, "And lead us not into temptation." Balanchine told her that he had been wrong to interfere with her marriage nine years before—a much older man hindering two young people. Farrell hardly knew what to say, but when Balanchine walked her home she could tell he felt more at peace.

Buoyed by this inner peace, Balanchine enthusiastically coached Baryshnikov in Villella's parts for the Saratoga season: *Rubies, Stars and Stripes, Coppélia, Afternoon of a Faun*. Next the company went on tour to Copenhagen, and Balanchine dragged his young countryman about in search of the perfect herring. Baryshnikov didn't have the heart to tell Balanchine that dancing with NYCB was stressing his muscles and joints more than expected. With the Kirov, Baryshnikov had performed once a week; with NYCB, eight times a week, in roles requiring speed and energy for which his training had not prepared him. He had arrived at his ultimate goal, dancing for Balanchine, but was not sure his body could keep him there.

Balanchine's body wasn't treating him so well, either. In Union Station after receiving the Kennedy Center Award in Washington, D.C., from President Jimmy Carter, he turned white and had to take a nitroglycerin pill, which stimulates heart activity. He rested into January 1979, then flew to Zurich to help Patricia Neary set *A Midsummer Night's Dream*, but he was too tired to enjoy the trip as usual. Back in New York his doctors told him he needed bypass surgery.

Uh-uh, said Balanchine at first. Not after that botched knee surgery 53 years before. He undertook a low-cholesterol diet and in April 1979 started setting *Le Bourgeois Gentilhomme* for the New York City Opera.

Rudolph Nureyev, the famed Soviet defector, was to dance the lead. For 18 years he had performed with major companies all over the world. He took every opportunity to dance a Balanchine ballet, but now was his first time working with the ballet master himself. He marveled when Balanchine choreographed backward from the ballet's high point toward the beginning, an inside-out process to which NYCB dancers were long accustomed. But he worried because Balanchine, rather than taking it easy, kept demonstrating the steps.

Balanchine's facility to demonstrate what he wanted was legendary. Right up into his 70s, his dancers would tell each other that they could never hope to do their roles as beautifully as Balanchine demonstrated them. By then, of course, he wasn't doing multiple turns or high jumps with beats. Yet he communicated energy and rhythm. With his head and arms and upper body he indicated focus, the direction of bodily bending, the intent of the music, and the challenge to go beyond perceived limits. "More, dear," he would say to his dancers, once remarking in company class, "And why more? Because more is always there" (98). His dancers responded to his high demand and unending patience with the beauty, speed, and musicality for which their company was famous.

Nureyev loved what he was seeing, but felt anxious for Mr. B's health. In one rehearsal he tried mild deception to slow the activity down: "Mr. Balanchine, I have to stand and figure out the counts" (99). Instead, Balanchine kept demonstrating, walked Nureyev to Madame Karinska's shop for a two-hour costume fitting, and then left for the evening's performance, where his dancers saw him as always in the downstage right wing.

Teaching Baryshnikov *Apollo* for the May 1979 season occupied Balanchine next. Rumor had it that Balanchine was changing that long-beloved work. When at last Baryshnikov performed it on May 1, the rumors were confirmed in cries of outrage. Not only had Balanchine removed the opening story showing Apollo's birth and maturing, but he, Mr. Born-to-Make-the-Music-Visible, had cut Stravinsky's score!

Letters to the editor and newspaper columns demanded the reason for this change. Balanchine responded that all he did was take out the garbage. "Dancing isn't about anything except dancing—everything else is boring," he snapped (100), and though he did later restore Apollo's first variation, he made it clear that his ballets were his to change. (Perhaps if his viewers had mounted the same ballet for 50 years, they'd have changed it too.)

About a month later, Baryshnikov hesitantly told him that ABT's founding director, Lucia Chase, was retiring and had offered him a major career opportunity: her job. Though it meant losing a wonderful dancer after only a year, Balanchine generously encouraged him to take it. Baryshnikov knew this decision was best; he had learned 22 roles with NYCB in 12 months, too fiery a pace to continue much longer.

By now Balanchine's angina (chest pains indicating low oxygen supply to the heart) became too severe to ignore. Lincoln Kirstein convinced him to have the bypass operation; it had restored Kirstein's health in 1975.

On the night before the surgery, NYCB doctor William Hamilton visited Balanchine. "You know," Balanchine said (though Hamilton had not asked), "I wasn't meant to marry Suzanne. It was God's decision" (101). It was plain that Farrell's departure in 1969 had been a central event in his life, that he had resolved his grief, disappointment, and outrage by trusting God, and that he felt able to trust his soul to God now.

The operation was successful. A month recovering in the hospital plus several weeks more of rest forced Balanchine to miss the Saratoga season for the first time. His dancers tried not to glance at the empty spot in the downstage right wing, but sometimes they danced through tears.

By September 1979 Balanchine was well enough to tour cheerfully with NYCB to London, recommending bypass surgery to everyone. Once back in New York, though, his friends quietly kept an eye on him. Eddie Bigelow stopped by his apartment most mornings, and Dr. Hamilton did so daily, usually finding Balanchine in his underwear at the ironing board, listening to classical music on the radio.

One day Balanchine's all's-well greeting to the doctor was absentminded. Instead of ironing a shirt, he was striding through his living room between piles of music scores written by 19th-century German composer Robert Alexander Schumann. The music was *Davidsbündlertänze* (Dance of the Leagues of David). For the first time in two years, Balanchine was choreographing.

He produced a brooding, dark-toned piece that fascinated his spring 1980 audiences. The choreography had each of five couples enter, dance, and exit without apparent awareness of the others, evoking a poignant sense of isolation amid emotions of tenderness, joy, and yearning. A live pianist onstage generated the music. In the final movement, Karin von Aroldingen gently placed Adam Lüders' hands on his own face and danced with him a little. Then, as sorrowfully as Schumann's wife Clara had watched her husband descend into madness, von Aroldingen watched Lüders back slowly away from her until the curtain fell.

At the *Robert Schumann's "Davidsbündlertänze"* premiere, the applause went on so insistently that Balanchine smilingly took four bows, holding hands with Suzanne Farrell on his right and von Aroldingen on his left.

Balanchine got to Saratoga that summer (though von Aroldingen showed up daily at his cottage to drive him wherever he might need). He also enjoyed the company's subsequent tour to Copenhagen, Paris, and Berlin. Back in New York, he visited the SAB workshop rehearsals, in which students were learning ballets for their yearly performance. One young lady named Darci Kistler stood out for her energy and concentration. Balanchine coached her in the demanding *Swan Lake* lead. While watching this 76-year-old heart patient demonstrate her steps, she discovered, as had so many before her, that "he put the fear of life into you. He'd show and run, full of energy and a kind of reality. He kind of dared you" (102). She absorbed the challenge and answered it with such drive that Balanchine took her into the company, and then promoted her at age 16 to become NYCB's youngest-ever principal.

In the midst of his renewed strength, Balanchine was about to endure a shock wave coming from a direction he could never have anticipated: his dancers.

More than most companies, the structure of NYCB was centered on its ballet master. In 1959, ballet historian Olga Maynard commented, "The most serious flaw in the character of the Company is its absolute dependence on Balanchine," even though she also saw NYCB as "remarkable for its stability, and the singleness of direction in its artistic policy" (103). In 1963, choreographer and historian Agnes de Mille noted that NYCB "became one of the leading ballet companies in the world. It is, however, entirely under the personal domination of Balanchine and bears the stamp of his personality and style" (104).

Not everyone saw Balanchine's dominance as a flaw. Daniel Duell remarked, "He was authoritarian, demanding great discipline, but not punitive . . . If you could see his intent, most of the time most of us committed to it" (105).

Perhaps the standout reason that the dancers fulfilled such rigorous demands was that Balanchine was no less demanding of himself. Not only did he produce hundreds of ballets, each requiring intense discipline to take from concept to production, but to the end of his life he was usually first to come to and last to leave the theater. More than one dancer or staff member who happened to be at the New York State Theater late at night saw him after everyone else had left, turning off lights to save electricity and cleaning cigarettes and chewing gum away from the studio pianos. During the performing seasons, the dancers knew exactly where to find Mr. B. every evening: in the downstage right wing or, at times, out in the audience.

Balanchine's health trials had altered that one-big-family atmosphere. Morning company class had been, in a sense, his daily meeting with his dancers. Not all attended every class, but during the course of each week Balanchine saw and spoke to almost every company dancer personally. Since his heart attack in March 1978 he had taught class less and less, and of course he had been forced to miss all too many performances. Dancers who had joined NYCB in the last three years barely knew him. And the company now numbered 105.

Thus Balanchine's personal influence over each dancer had diminished, and meanwhile, outside influences had been at work. One example was the near-strike at American Ballet Theatre. The high yearly salaries accorded to foreign principal dancers such as Russian star Alexander Godunov contrasted painfully with the minimal increase in corps pay in the new ABT contracts. Hearing that its dancers might go on strike, the ABT management locked them out.

Such difficulties had never been encountered at NYCB, where Balanchine had abolished the star system, and salaries were much more fair. Nonetheless, some newer NYCB dancers began to point out that dancers still earned less than garbage men, and less overall than NYCB orchestra musicians (whose career was quite demanding: they played some of the world's most difficult music while obscured in the orchestra pit). These dancers' protest was ironic because at that time they had by far the best contracts of any AGMA dancers. Daniel Duell, the NYCB delegate for AGMA, had carefully worked with Betty Cage in 1976 to negotiate salaries that rose 56 percent by 1980—a most unusually high increase—as well as providing better vacation pay and a structure for corps pay so that fifth-year corps members (who were usually about 23 years old) would earn the same as starting NYCB orchestra members (who had to attend college and start full-time work at about age 23). The NYCB dancers could take classes free at SAB and had a home theater in which to perform. Dancers in other companies had no base school and had to pay for their classes out of their salaries. They also had no home theater. When the NYCB contract was up for renegotiation in 1980, Duell and Cage put in long extra hours reorganizing its many sections because the standard AGMA format made the contract hard to comprehend. Meanwhile, Balanchine and the NYCB board members met at various times with groups of dancers to give all issues a hearing.

In light of these facts, it was particularly unfit that during a poorly attended AGMA union meeting, the NYCB dancers present voted 26 to 18 to strike for more pay.

Outraged and grieved upon hearing this news, Balanchine called a meeting for December 23, 1980, after company class. All 105 dancers attended. Quietly he told them that he and Kirstein could not offer more than the current salary plan, which would continue to raise dancer pay gradually over the next three years. If they struck, so be it, but he could not accept a strike on which hardly half had even voted. If need be, he and Kirstein could raise up a new company somewhere else. "I want a vote for myself and I don't give a damn if it's illegal!" he concluded. "Yes or no from a hundred and five!" (106). He exited, leaving a box into which all 105 dancers could cast their votes.

Duell and his brother, principal dancer Joseph Duell, carefully structured the revote process so that all the dancers' names would be accounted for without revealing who chose for or against. The strike was overwhelmingly voted down. Nonetheless, it was now plain that Balanchine's single-handed control over his growing organization was unwieldy and vulnerable to his health troubles. Once again and more urgently the issue of succession arose. Who would care for NYCB if Balanchine became unable to do it?

Balanchine had fielded such questions at least since 1973. At times he deflected them by saying that, being Georgian, he would live to age 135. At other times, he would say that of course if he died someone else would take over and NYCB would become a different company. What could be more natural? Meanwhile, he was still alive and, to use Darci Kistler's words, "full of energy and a kind of reality." His earthly body had its own reality that was conflicting with Balanchine's inner vision, but until the earthly reality won out, he had visions to make visible.

Chapter 10
Beyond the Potato Patch (1980–1983)

Balanchine was famous for not explaining his ballets.

"What's this ballet about?" someone might ask, and he would respond, "Oh, about 20 minutes." Then he would produce a piece that would stir viewers' profoundest emotions for the next 50 years and beyond.

Of course, each Balanchine ballet had a central focus. Nonetheless, what each ballet was "about" was not just that focus; it was "about" what he and his dancers together discovered when working with the music. Balanchine was the absolute leader, the primogenitor of his ballets, but it was with his dancers that he worked his ideas into marvels of intricate timing within groups, of variations on themes, of a soloist flashing through a corps immersed in motion, of a man and woman doing spins and leaps interspersed with a loving handclasp or a poignant touch of hand to cheek. In every ballet, he introduced movements specific to it that reappeared in various ways throughout the piece. No computer could map all the ways in which these variations coordinated, surprised, colluded, and reunited the movement themes.

Given Mr. B's ability to set dances *with* his dancers as much as *on* them, perhaps it is no wonder that Frank Ohman, an NYCB soloist for 22 years who started his own school and company in 1983, called Balanchine's ballets *fun*: "They were always so musical. It just all fit so well. It wasn't like, oh, heck, I gotta do this. No! I loved to dance and his ballets were so much fun to do" (107).

Some people accused Balanchine's dancers of not showing emotion. Perhaps these accusers were applying inappropriate theater precepts to ballet. For Balanchine, dancers' faces ideally reflected the mood of a piece, but were not the medium through which the ideas flowed. He once told a French interviewer, in his Russian-influenced French, *"C'est pas emotion; c'est motion"*—it's not emotion, it's motion (108). When audiences saw Balanchine's choreography, they saw his ideas about life.

Balanchine had explored joyful relationships as well as unfulfilled love and spiritual yearning in many of his ballets. Now he explored death, not by making dancers act as if they were dying, but by representing the spiritual meaning of life and death. As usual, he said little about his intentions to his dancers and even less to his audience. But they all got the idea.

This exploration first manifested itself through the Tchaikovsky Festival that Balanchine and Jerome Robbins mounted in late spring 1981. Two of the four ballets Balanchine created were upbeat: *Hungarian Gypsy Airs* and the Garland Dance from *The Sleeping Beauty*. The other two pointed beyond earthly life: *Mozartiana* and *Adagio Lamentoso*.

Mozartiana was Tchaikovsky's arrangement of a group of pieces written by Wolfgang Amadeus Mozart. Balanchine had used the music before; now he made something new. Suzanne Farrell and four young SAB girls danced the opening section, called "Preghiera," the Italian word for prayer. Its melody was Mozart's *Ave Verum*, which is Latin for "Hail, True." The *Ave Verum* is a prayer spoken in the Roman Catholic liturgy, and it refers to Jesus' death on the cross to redeem the sins of the world. Balanchine began the first rehearsal of "Preghiera" by asking Farrell to recite the prayer. Having been raised Roman Catholic, she knew it by heart. She hummed it to herself as she danced the choreography, using the words as her cues rather than the musical counts. Farrell saw this segment as "a hymn shared by George and me, an offering that could happen only in movement and music, not in words" (109). The rest of the choreography for *Mozartiana* was light-hearted, including a duet with variations for Farrell and a fine young Danish dancer named Ib Andersen. But all 11 dancers in it wore black, though Farrell's long black tutu was edged with white.

Adagio Lamentoso, the other piece that pointed to immortal life, closed the entire festival. Its music was the 1893 Symphony No. 6, also known as the *Pathetique*. Symphonies have several sections called movements. Usually the last movement is upbeat. However, the last movement of *Pathetique* was adagio (slow) and ended with deep mournful notes on a stringed instrument that faded into silence. Also, *Pathetique* included in its first movement some of the melody sung at a Russian Orthodox requiem, or service for the dead. Balanchine was sure Tchaikovsky composed the piece knowing of his own impending death, which occurred nine days after the symphony's 1893 premiere.

Though Karin von Aroldingen had a foot injury at the time, Balanchine asked that she lead *Adagio Lamentoso* because, he said, "You are the one person who knows how to mourn" (110). She led a group of women walking across the stage as if looking for comfort. Angels with white wings sweeping high above their heads entered protectively and then watchfully surrounded the back of the stage. Hooded figures in purple and red disturbed the women, but then monks hooded in black processed in and lay face down so that their bodies shaped a cross onstage. Balanchine used a mundane, ordinary men's exercise—pushups—to absolutely remarkable effect: the monks pushed themselves up and let themselves down at differing levels, in slow, smooth rhythm with the mournful notes of the *Pathetique* final movement. To the watching audience, the huge black cross seemed to pulse, as if embodying the fading beats of a human heart. A small boy walked on wearing a white gown and carrying a candle. The last notes of music diminished into silence; the monks' motion ceased; the little boy blew his candle out, leaving the stage and the entire auditorium in thick darkness.

Too stunned to applaud, the audience quietly left the theater.

Balanchine broke his own silence about what his ballets meant the next day. He told *New York Times* critic Anna Kisselgoff that the boy with the candle represented a pure soul. Balanchine quoted a parable from the Sufi Muslim religion of Turkey: A man asks a small boy with a candle to explain where the candle's light comes from. The boy blows the candle out, replying that if the man can tell him where the light has gone, he will tell the man where it came from.

Kisselgoff articulated in her column how personally and powerfully Balanchine had united the worlds of the visible and the invisible with his tribute to Tchaikovsky. She called *Adagio Lamentoso* "a daring, disturbing and moving way to end the Tchaikovsky Festival" (111). Three weeks later another very influential dance critic named Jack Anderson called *Lamentoso* "a solemn, disquieting ballet about the transitoriness of life and the inevitability of death" (112).

Balanchine startled a friend over lunch not long after the festival by saying he could not waste time on unimportant matters because he only had two more years to live. But he seemed lively and well for the 1981 Saratoga season. During a trip overseas, he attended a ball for Princess Grace of Monaco. Barbara Horgan and Karin von Aroldingen came too. In response to waltz music, Balanchine offered a hand to Karin—the hand that had so many times led her to the center of the studio floor to start a new ballet. His snow-white hair, prominent cheekbones, and slightly hunched shoulders contradicted the youthful grace of his expression. Everyone at the ball watched, entranced, as the two waltzed, but von Aroldingen could tell Balanchine was more than ready to sit down when the music ended.

By December 1981 he was having moments when he would turn gray and have trouble talking. By spring 1982 he kept hearing loud roars and clatters in his head. Neurological tests could not determine why, nor explain Balanchine's occasional loss of balance. He hated having to use a cane, and instead carried a large umbrella to steady himself.

Nonetheless he rallied the company around a Stravinsky festival, to celebrate what would have been the composer's 100th birthday. In addition it would celebrate the company that performed more Stravinsky ballets than any other, not to mention the acclaimed NYCB orchestra, which had played more Stravinsky than any other orchestra.

Despite his increasing physical limitations, Balanchine once again generated a happy universe around himself and his project. In fact, he united universes past and present. Francisco Moncion came back to perform in a restaging of the 1962 television production *Noah and the Flood*. Robert Craft returned to conduct *Noah* and Jacques d'Amboise helped stage it. Vera Zorina flew in to do the spoken parts of *Perséphone*, Stravinsky's musical drama about a Greek goddess. Balanchine also rechoreographed two solos for Suzanne Farrell: *Élegie* and *Variations for Orchestra*. In *Tango*, he assigned 40-year-old Karin von Aroldingen to partner 20-year-old Christopher d'Amboise, evoking wry laughs when he mischievously told Jacques to understudy his son.

It all sort of worked. Balanchine said nary a word about the pain in his joints and muscles, the noises in his head, or the glaucoma and cataracts dimming his eyesight. He was gracious and patient when, unsuccessfully trying to find a free studio in which to rehearse *Variations* with Farrell, the two of them ended up clearing music stands from an orchestra rehearsal room and rehearsing on its slick linoleum. But his concentration was deteriorating. Jacques d'Amboise had to finish *Noah*. John Taras had to rescue *Persephone*. The Stravinsky Centennial was Balanchine's last big project.

The succeeding months of 1982 were hard. Balanchine's increasingly unsteady balance kept him confined to his cottage during the Saratoga season; he didn't make it to the theater once. In August he submitted to cataract surgery. How disappointed he was when his improved vision did not result in steadier legs! His mystified doctors looked on in frustration as their uncomplaining patient worsened. He had to hire a live-in nurse to help with his daily self-care needs.

In early November, Balanchine cooked a roast beef dinner at his apartment for Patricia Neary and Barbara Horgan. He loved to cook. Every Easter he would invite special friends for a traditional Russian meal, complete with homemade *kulitch* bread and *pascha* cheese dessert. He would recall preparing family meals by his mother's side before getting enrolled in the Imperial School, and he often likened choreography to creating a beautiful repast.

On this late autumn night, however, he had to excuse himself at the early hour of 7:30 P.M. The next morning, right in front of Barbara Horgan and the nurse, he fell and cracked several ribs. Patricia Neary arrived and he saw in her face how bad he looked compared to the previous night. With both sorrow and relief the three women listened as he thanked them for their care and told them they had done all they could for him. On November 4, 1982, Dr. Hamilton admitted him to Roosevelt Hospital for observation.

Balanchine's telephone became his conduit for running the company from his hospital room. But as the weeks passed, his mind increasingly lost function. He would call the theater during performance time, and when someone answered, confusedly ask for Karin.

His many visitors would enter his room not knowing whether he might be alert, or so ill he could only give them a smile and a hug. A Russian teacher at SAB, Andrei Kramarevsky, would sit on his bed, chatting in Russian, choking up when Balanchine told him, "Oh, now is a terrible time. I can't go and cook" (113).

On January 22, 1983, Balanchine turned 79 years old. Karin von Aroldingen prepared 79 Russian meatballs, made the way Balanchine had taught her, and brought them to his hospital room. About 20 close friends accompanied her. Sadly, within the hour, everyone had to acknowledge that Balanchine was too ill to enjoy the celebration. Tearfully they kissed him and tiptoed out.

Visitors continued to come as the days passed, and Balanchine continued to decline. His eyes lit up when he heard Karin von Aroldingen's step; she came most frequently and stayed the longest. His memory became so unreliable that after she got home from a visit he would sometimes call her house and ask when she was coming to see him.

Balanchine told Dr. Hamilton about the wonderful music and beautiful dances he could envision. When Dr. Hamilton asked how he thought all those dances up, Balanchine said he just had dancers in the studio do the things that came into his mind. Pointing upward, Balanchine explained, "He tells me" (114).

Vera Zorina was able to come several times during the six months Balanchine was in the hospital, feeding him crumbs of very soft chocolate or sharing a miniature sip of champagne. At her last visit, he could only clutch her hand with the instinctive strength of an infant, clasping a crucifix that hung on a ribbon around his neck with his other hand; she wordlessly stroked his hair. At home that night she wept, knowing she would not see him again.

On March 15, 1983, five years to the day after Balanchine's first heart attack, a statement from the NYCB Board of Directors was read to the assembled dancers and staff: Peter Martins and Jerome Robbins were named joint ballet-masters-in-chief of the New York City Ballet. Balanchine had been named Ballet Master Emeritus. The unthinkable had become reality. There would be no more new Balanchine ballets.

On April 24, Karin von Aroldingen heard Balanchine's last spoken words: he murmured for her to come and see him any time. On Saturday, April 30, 1983, at 4:00 A.M., he breathed his last.

It was a tribute to Balanchine that on the day he died, so much was happening at the school and theater. The students of the School of American Ballet danced *Valse Fantasie* and *Western Symphony* that afternoon in the Juilliard Theater for the annual SAB workshop performance, with members of Nancy LaSalle's advisory committee in from all over the country to watch. The NYCB spring season had started; Karin von Aroldingen was scheduled to dance *Kammermusik No. 2* for the afternoon matinee, and she did it in a state of numbness. Like the other dancers tearfully warming up, Peter Martins and Suzanne Farrell had to decide whether they could perform the adagio movement of *Symphony in C* that evening without dissolving into grief. They all knew unquestionably that Balanchine would want them to. As Daniel Duell later commented, "We all felt that we must give of ourselves ultimately to show people that though Mr. B has left this earth, he is very much alive" (115).

Before each of the performances that Saturday, Lincoln Kirstein stepped in front of the curtain with Jerome Robbins, Peter Martins, and John Taras. Kirstein told the audience, "I don't have to tell you that Mr. B. is with Mozart and Tchaikovsky and Stravinsky." He explained that Mr. B. would desire most of all for his beloved company to perform without interruption, and concluded, "Think of yourselves as the marvelous, supportive, cohesive family who understands the family that's about to perform now" (116). Thus audience and dancers endured sorrow together by participating in Balanchine's world of beauty.

Serge Diaghilev would have rejoiced to see the tributes to his protégé in newspapers throughout the United States and Europe. New York City Mayor Edward I. Koch issued a statement in which he called Balanchine "the acknowledged master of ballet of the 20th century" (117).

As the staff and dancers of the New York City Ballet emerged from the first weeks of grief, there were decisions to be made. Balanchine was not wealthy. In his will, his physical and financial property had been simple enough to divide among those closest to him: Karin von Aroldingen, Barbara Horgan, and Tanaquil Le Clerq. He did not forget his brother Andrei, but left him two gold watches that Lincoln Kirstein had given him.

His ballets, which legally were called his *intellectual property*, were another matter. Who had riches to compare with Balanchine's? Stravinsky, perhaps, or Tchaikovsky.

While Balanchine was alive, he held the legal rights to his ballets. No one could legally perform a Balanchine ballet without his permission, and he decided whether to charge money for the privilege of using his work. Now that he had died, the rights to the ballets became a legal issue. Balanchine had foreseen this problem. To the press and to others who bothered him about the future of his ballets, he used to say he didn't care what happened to the ballets after he died. But he cared very much about the people in his life, and it was to these people that he willed about 100 of the ballets he thought worthy of continuing performance. Most of these people were dancers. To Suzanne Farrell, for example, he left *Tzigane* and *Don Quixote*. Patricia McBride received the rights to *Tarantella* and two other ballets. Because Balanchine was concerned for the financial well-being of Tanaquil Le Clercq, she received the rights to more ballets than anyone else.

When a person dies, the property he or she designates in a will to be left to another is called a *bequest*. Balanchine's bequests of money, property, and ballets were to those whom he named in his will. But what he bequeathed to his dancers and his public—past, present, and future—was much more than money, property, or even ballets.

He bequeathed the courage of innovation. Like Marius Petipa in the 19th century, like Fokine and Goleizovsky in the early 20th, Balanchine honored artistic tradition by adding to it—perhaps only very aged dancers can understand how *much* he added. He refused to listen to his detractors, but listened instead to his unique ideas, and then went to the immense trouble to make them real. And he constantly encouraged others to do the same.

Through his unique visions, he bequeathed the ability to commit to something wonderful. Principal dancer Merrill Ashley commented on Balanchine's belief in his work: "Ballet is something that must be highly respected, treated with great care and not mistreated . . . a noble pursuit, noble and dignified" (118).

As part of that pursuit, he bequeathed a respectful working environment. Former NYCB member Richard Tanner said, "In other ballet companies there's so much temperament. . . . But not at New York City Ballet. When people realize that kind of behavior isn't tolerated, nobody thinks it's glamorous or interesting" (119).

An important facet of this respectful environment was conflict management. Within any group, disputes can arise over choreography, or any other matter. Then factions that oppose each other can form. The unity is damaged and the work does not get done. Balanchine derailed disputes by refocusing the dancers on the work: "There is not to be public drama during rehearsal, so we'll deal with this later," he would say. If the issue was correct choreography, he would announce, "Whatever it was, now will be this," and terminate the argument by redefining the steps himself. Results mattered, not petty squabbles about who was more right than whom (120).

Through his kindness, generosity, and respect, his humor, his encouragement, and his steady presence, Balanchine bequeathed love. Men's wardrobe supervisor Leslie Copeland said frankly, "He was always surrounded by love. And he gave love as well" (121). It was not only Balanchine's strong authority that held the company together, not only his commitment or his creative genius, but his love for those who worked with him.

And he bequeathed integrity. Art speaks about life. Serious artists try to communicate what they believe is true. The great ballet master died with little monetary wealth to his name because he decided not to compromise his artistic vision. Even when critics sneered or viewers misunderstood, he produced the truest, most beautiful, most inventive choreography he could, and he addressed the highest ideals of the heart.

Balanchine knew where every gift lodged in his person came from. "I am a waiter—for God," he told biographer Bernard Taper. "We are all servants of God, or destiny, whatever you wish to call it. I am not so proud, and I am not so great—I'm nothing but what He has wanted me to be" (122). In accepting his servanthood, he left the world around him enriched with heavenly treasure.

Illustrations

1: Ballet has five basic positions of the feet, plus arm positions associated with the foot positions. This page shows (top to bottom) first position, front and profile; second position, front and profile, third position, front only. Third position of the feet is used only by early beginners, but third position of the arms is used frequently in class work and choreography. Drawings ©Reine Duell Bethany.

2: Top row: fourth position of the feet, front and profile, showing variations in the arm positions associated with fourth. Bottom row: fifth position, front and profile. When the arms are curved downward, the arm position is called fifth low; up, fifth high. Drawings ©Reine Duell Bethany.

3: The top three dancers are doing movements that are variations of second position, shown by the bottom figure. The bottom figure is standing in a position called tendú á la seconde par terre (foot extended toward second position with toe touching the floor) Drawings ©Reine Duell Bethany.

4: Variations on first arabesque. "Arabesque," meaning "Arab-ish," refers to Arabic script, admired for its swooping, graceful lines. In ballet, "arabesque" always means that one leg is pointed strongly back, making a long, lovely line.

Ballet has five main arabesque positions, named for where the arms are held and how the dancer's body is oriented toward the audience. Basic first arabesque par terre is shown at bottom; the upper three figures show variations. Drawings © Reine Duell Bethany. The male dancer is NYCB principal Joseph Duell, a detail drawing from the original photo by Martha Swope/©The New York Public Library.

5: The three Balanchivadze children, left to right: Tamara, Georgi, Andrei. Photographer unknown. © The George Balanchine Trust. Courtesy of the New York City Ballet.

6: Balanchine (seated) with brother Andrei wearing their Imperial School uniforms. Photographer unknown. ©The George Balanchine Trust. Courtesy of the New York City Ballet.

7: *Agon* rehearsal. NYCB principals Arthur Mitchell and Diana Adams in foreground. Balanchine and Stravinsky are seated, watching. Photo by Martha Swope/© The New York Public Library. Courtesy of the New York City Ballet.

8: Balanchine conducts a teaching seminar, c. 1960. Photographer unknown. ©The George Balanchine Trust. Courtesy of the New York City Ballet.

9: Lincoln Kirstein and George Balanchine seated in rehearsal studio, early 1960s. Photo by Martha Swope/© The New York Public
Library. Courtesy of the New York City Ballet.

10: *A Midsummer Night's Dream* rehearsal, mid 1960s. Principal dancer Edward Villella stands behind Balanchine, who is kissing the hand of Suzanne Farrell. Conrad Ludlow, NYCB principal who originated important Balanchine roles, is at right. Photo by Martha Swope/© The New York Public Library. Courtesy of the New York City Ballet.

11: 1972 *Pulcinella* rehearsal, male cast, with Balanchine and Jerome Robbins. NYCB principal Daniel Duell is directly behind
Balanchine. Photo by Martha Swope/© The New York Public Library. Courtesy of the New York City Ballet.

12: Curtain call after performance of *Coppélia*, 1974. Balanchine with NYCB Orchestra Conductor Robert Irving, NYCB principals Helgi Tomasson, Patricia McBride, and Colleen Neary, and Alexandra Danilova. Photo by Martha Swope/© The New York Public Library. Courtesy of the New York City Ballet.

13: 1977 rehearsal of *Vienna Waltzes*. Balanchine is watching
NYCB principals Kay Mazzo and Peter Martins. Their calm concentration reflects the tempest-free, efficient creativity of a Balanchine rehearsal. Photo by Martha Swope/© The New York Public
Library. Courtesy of the New York City Ballet.

14: Balanchine in motion during a 1977 *Vienna Waltzes* rehearsal. His idea is reflected both in his own motion and in the swirl of Karin von Aroldingen's skirt, while her partner for *Waltzes*, NYCB principal Sean Lavery, looks on. Photo by Martha Swope/© The New York Public Library. Courtesy of the New York City Ballet.

15: "I don't have to tell you that Mr. B. is with Mozart and Tchaikovsky and Stravinsky." Drawing © Reine Duell Bethany, 2012.

16: Balanchine contemplates his audience during one of his rare bows after a performance. Photograph: © Steven Caras. This photo is owned and copyrighted by Steven Caras, All Rights Reserved.

Balanchine Time Line

January 22, 1904
Georgi Melitonovich Balanchivadze born in St. Petersburg, Russia.

1913
At age 9, accepted into ballet section of St. Petersburg Imperial School of Theatre and Ballet.

c. 1915
Appears with other children in Maryinsky Theatre production of *Sleeping Beauty;* decides to dedicate his life to ballet.

1917
Fall of the Romanov empire. Bolshevik takeover. Imperial School closes. Georgi moves in with his aunt and struggles against starvation.

c. 1918
Maryinsky Theatre reopens as the State Theater of Opera and Ballet. Georgi and other students return to life at the ballet school.

c. 1919
Georgi begins to choreograph. In late 1920, performs his first piece, a pas de deux (dance for two) called *La Nuit,* to music by Russian composer Anton Rubenstein.

1921
Graduates Petrograd Imperial Theatre School, with honors. Joins State Theatre ballet company as a corps member. Enrolls in Petrograd conservatory of music and trains in musical theory and piano for the next three years.

1922–1923

Marries Tamara Geva. Assembles his own troupe, the Young Ballet, and produces several evenings of repertory that includes his own choreography. Mixed reviews. Not well received by dance authorities.

1924

With Tamara Geva, Alexandra Danilova, and Nicholas Efimov under Vladimir Dimitriev, goes on European tour as Soviet State Dancers. Once in Germany, all decide not to return to Russia. Serge Diaghilev hires them in Paris to dance with Ballets Russes. Georgi Balanchivadze changed to George Balanchine.

1925

Diaghilev appoints Balanchine ballet master (main choreographer) of Ballets Russes.

1926

Marriage to Tamara Geva fails. Ballerina Alexandra Danilova becomes his common-law wife.

1927

Knee injury ends Balanchine's performing except for character roles.

1928

Choreographs *Apollon Musagète* (later renamed *Apollo*), to music by Igor Stravinsky. Lifelong collaboration and friendship with Stravinsky is established.

1929

Choreographs *Prodigal Son,* which is viewed in Paris by a young American arts patron, Lincoln Kirstein. Serge Diaghilev dies; Ballets Russes folds. Balanchine almost dies of tuberculosis; recovers, but is left with only one lung fully functional.

1930–1933
Balanchine finds work choreographing for several European groups, from classical ballet to vaudeville. Helps form the Ballet Russe de Monte Carlo, but is fired by its director, Col. W. de Basil.

1933
Lincoln Kirstein convinces Balanchine and Balanchine's manager, Vladimir Dimitriev, to migrate to the United States for the purpose of establishing a ballet school and company.

January 2, 1934
The School of American Ballet holds its first classes at 637 Madison Avenue.

Spring 1934
Balanchine choreographs *Serenade* for the students, which is presented in June.

1934–1939
Balanchine choreographs extensively for ballet, opera, Broadway, and film. In 1938, he marries ballerina Vera Zorina. In 1939, he becomes a U.S. citizen.

1941
Nelson Rockefeller, serving under President F. D. Roosevelt as Coordinator of Inter-American Affairs, asks Balanchine to do a goodwill tour of South America. Balanchine and Kirstein in response assemble American Ballet Caravan; Balanchine choreographs *Concerto Barocco* and *Ballet Imperial* (later renamed *Tchaikovsky Piano Concerto No.2*).

1942–1944
Kirstein and male dancers drafted to fight in World War II. Balanchine decreases musical theater work and increases ballet work.

1944–1946

Ballet master for the Ballet Russe de Monte Carlo, which is no longer under de Basil and now tours the United States.

1946

Balanchine and Zorina divorce. He marries Ballet Russe ballerina Maria Tallchief. Kirstein and Balanchine form Ballet Society, a ballet company supported by subscriptions and private donations and devoted to Balanchine's vision of ballet. Balanchine restages *L'Enfant et les Sortilèges* and choreographs Paul Hindemith's *The Four Temperaments*.

1947

Balanchine creates *Le Palais de Cristal* for the Paris Opéra Ballet. This work is later renamed *Symphony in C.* Performances of Ballet Society continue.

1948

Choreographs *Orpheus* for Ballet Society. Morton Baum, chairman of finance committee for City Center, where Ballet Society performs, sees *Orpheus* and offers to make Ballet Society a publicly supported institution called the New York City Ballet. Balanchine and Kirstein accept. The New York City Ballet is born.

1949

Balanchine choreographs *Firebird*, featuring Maria Tallchief.

1950

First NYCB foreign tour (six weeks at Covent Garden in London). Jerome Robbins joins NYCB as dancer, choreographer, and subsequently, associate director.

1951

Balanchine choreographs *La Valse* for Tanaquil Le Clerq, excerpts of which appear in the first commercial color television broadcast by CBS.

1952

Balanchine choreographs *Scotch Symphony.* Marriage to Maria Tallchief annulled. On December 31, Balanchine marries Tanaquil Le Clerq.

1954

Choreographs *Western Symphony.* Also choreographs NYCB's first full evening-length ballet, *The Nutcracker.*

1956

Choreographs *Allegro Brillante.* NYCB goes on European tour. In Copenhagen, Le Clerq suffers an attack of polio and is permanently paralyzed from the waist down.

1957

Balanchine promotes NYCB's first African American dancer, Arthur Mitchell. For Mitchell and ballerina Diana Adams, Balanchine choreographs *Agon,* another turning point in Balanchine's choreographic progress, and the notable because an African American man partners a white ballerina onstage.

First Ford Foundation scholarships offered to help scout talent across America.

Suzanne Farrell becomes a Ford Foundation Scholarship student at SAB.

1958

Balanchine institutes alphabetical listing of principals, soloists, and corps, rejecting star treatment of any dancers. Choreographs *Stars and Stripes* and *The Seven Deadly Sins.*

1959

Collaborates with modern dance pioneer Martha Graham to set *Episodes.*

1960

Choreographs *Tchaikovsky Pas de Deux* and *Liebeslieder Walzer.* Initiates free Saturday afternoon matinee performances at City Center for public school students.

1962

Choreographs another full-length ballet, *A Midsummer Night's Dream.*

NYCB tours Europe, including five weeks in Russia. Balanchine sees his younger brother Andrei for the first time in 43 years.

1964

On April 23, NYCB moves into its new home, the New York State Theater in the newly constructed Lincoln Center in midtown Manhattan.

1965

Balanchine choreographs *Don Quixote,* NYCB's third full-length ballet, featuring Suzanne Farrell as Dulcinea. Balanchine courts Farrell.

1966

Saratoga Performing Arts Center in Saratoga Springs, New York, is completed. NYCB debuts there on July 8, inaugurating a yearly summer season.

1967

Balanchine choreographs *Jewels,* the first full-length plotless ballet. Danish premier danseur Peter Martins performs with NYCB on tour and starts guesting with company.

1969

Balanchine divorces Le Clerq in hope of marrying Farrell. But Farrell marries NYCB dancer Paul Mejia and the couple leaves NYCB.

1970

Balanchine premieres *Who Cares?* and receives the Handel Medallion, New York City's most coveted cultural award, from New York Mayor John Lindsay.

1971

Igor Stravinsky dies at age 88.

1972

Balanchine stages a week-long Stravinsky Festival, premiering (among many other works) *Duo Concertant, Stravinsky Violin Concerto,* and *Symphony in Three Movements.*

1974

Farrell returns to NYCB and remains until she retires from performing in 1989.

1976

Balanchine and Danilova collaborate to produce another full-length ballet, a staging of the famous European story ballet *Coppélia.* Balanchine choreographs *Union Jack,* a tribute to Great Britain during the American bicentennial.

1977

Balanchine choreographs V*ienna Waltzes.* In December, the Public Broadcasting Service airs "Choreography by Balanchine," a six-part presentation of his works, on its *Dance in America* series.

1978
Balanchine choreographs *Ballo della Regina.* Suffers a mild heart attack and writes a will. Becomes one of the first five recipients of the Kennedy Center Honors, presented by President Jimmy Carter.

1979
Undergoes heart bypass surgery.

1980
Choreographs *Robert Schumann's "Davidsbündlertänze."* Receives the Gold Medal of Merit from the National Society of Arts and Letters; the Austrian Cross of Honor for Science and Letters, First Class, from the Austrian government; and the Heart of New York award from the New York Chapter of the American Heart Association.

1981
Stages a two-week Tchaikovsky Festival, which features 12 new ballets. Choreographs *Adagio Lamentoso* and *Mozartiana.*

1982
Experiences increasing ill health and loss of balance. Enters Roosevelt Hospital on November 4, where he remains for the next five months, unable to go to Washington, D.C., to receive the Presidential Medal of Freedom that is awarded him in February 1983.

April 30, 1983
George Balanchine dies at age 79.

Endnotes

These endnotes reference the direct quotes that are correspondingly numbered throughout my text.

(1) Danilova, Alexandra. *Choura: The Memoirs of Alexandra Danilova.* New York: Knopf, 1986. 33.

(2) Taper, Bernard. *Balanchine: A Biography.* New York: Harper & Row, 1963. 79, 83.

(3) Danilova, 117.

(4) Taper, Bernard. *Balanchine: A Biography.* New York: Times Books, 1984. 91.

(5) Both quotes are from: Balanchine, George, and Francis Mason. *Balanchine's Complete Stories of the Great Ballets.* Revised and enlarged edition. Garden City, NY: Doubleday, 1977. 779.

(6) Haggin, B. H. *Discovering Balanchine.* New York: Horizon Press, 1981. 9.

(7) Danilova, 103.

(8) Taper 1963, 127–128.

(9) Markova, Dame Alicia. *Markova Remembers.* London: H. Hamilton, 1986. 19.

(10) Taper 1984, 128.

(11) Duberman, Martin. *The Worlds of Lincoln Kirstein.* New York: Knopf, 2007. 178.

(12) Smith, Sid. "Ballet Chicago's Balanchine Full of Thrills." *Chicago Tribune*, May 15, 2011. Web. Accessed May 16, 2011, and May 6, 2012, at http://articles.chicagotribune.com/2011-05-15/entertainment/ct-live-0516-balanchine-celebration-20110515_1_ted-seymour-rachel-jambois-george-balanchine-trust.

(13) Zorina, Vera. *Zorina.* New York: Farrar, Strauss, Giroux, 1986. 13.

(14) Zorina, 119.

(15) Zorina, 176–177.

(16) Zorina, 176–177.

(17) Taper 1963, 189.

(18) Buckle, Richard. *George Balanchine: Ballet Master.* With John Taras. New York: Random House, 1988. 118–119.

(19) Zorina, 202.

(20) Taper 1984, 195.

(21) Zorina, 249.

(22) Duberman, 360.

(23) Buckle, 146.

(24) Tracy, Robert, with Sharon DeLano. *Balanchine's Ballerinas: Conversations with the Muses.* New York: Linden Press/Simon & Schuster, 1983. 72.

(25) Anderson, Jack. "The One and Only: The Ballet Russe de Monte Carlo. The Balanchine Years." *Ballet Review* 8, no. 4 (1980): 311–352.

(26) Anderson 314.

(27) Taper 1984, 204.

(28) Duberman 409.

(29) Duberman 409.

(30) Taper 1984, 207.

(31) Taper 1984, 212.

(32) Mason, Francis. *I Remember Balanchine: Recollections of the Ballet Master by Those Who Knew Him.* New York: Doubleday, 1991. 258.

(33) Mason, 239.

(34) Taper 1984, 226.

(35) Taper 1984, 225, quoting Martins' article in the *New York Times,* April 29, 1948.

(36) Taper 1984, 225.

(37) Buckle, 181.

(38) Buckle, 181.

(39) Taper 1984, 230.

(40) Fisher, Barbara Milberg. *In Balanchine's Company: A Dancer's Memoir.* Middletown, CT: Wesleyan University Press, 2006. 15–16.

(41) Gruen, John. *The Private World of Ballet.* New York: Viking Press, 1975. 284.

(42) Gruen, 284.

(43) Mason, 291.

(44) Fisher, 142.

(45) Balanchine and Mason, 13.

(46) Balanchine and Mason, 14.

(47) Tracy, 116.

(48) Fisher, 156.

(49) Tracy, 120.

(50) Villella, Edward. *Prodigal Son: Dancing for Balanchine in a World of Pain and Magic.* With Larry Kaplan. New York: Simon and Schuster, 1992. 50.

(51) Buckle, 213.

(52) Fisher, 170.

(53) Villella, 50.

(54) Gruen, 444.

(55) Taper 1984, 248.

(56) Villella, 78.

(57) Mason, 148–149.

(58) de Mille, Agnes. *The Book of the Dance.* New York: Golden Press, 1963. 183.

(59) Taper 1984, 278.

(60) Buckle, 232–233.

(61) Buckle, 236.

(62) Buckle, 240.

(63) Buckle, 240–241.

(64) Farrell, Suzanne. *Holding On to the Air: An Autobiography.* With Toni Bentley. New York: Summit Books, 1990. p. 78.

(65) Farrell, 77–78.

(66) Villella, 143–144.

(67) Farrell, 93–94.

(68) Martins, Peter. *Far from Denmark.* Boston: Little, Brown, 1982. p. 91.

(69) Tracy, 193.

(70) Daniel Duell, personal interview with the author, January 2, 2012.

(71) Tracy, 116.

(72) Farrell, 125.

(73) Farrell, 109.

(74) Buckle, 248.

(75) Villella, 168.

(76) Farrell, 139.

(77) Gruen, John. *The Private World of Ballet.* New York: Viking Press, 1975. 283.

(78) Gruen, 294.

(79) Farrell, 182–183.

(80) Vaill, Amanda. *Somewhere: The Life of Jerome Robbins.* New York: Broadway Books, 2006. 405.

(81) Gruen, 244–245.

(82) Mason, *I Remember Balanchine*, 389.

(83) Buckle, 270.

(84) de Mille, 322–323.

(85) Mason, 416–417.

(86) Buckle, 272.

(87) Farrell, 230.

(88) Taper 1984, 321.

(89) Daniel Duell, personal interview, January 2, 2012.

(90) Daniel Duell, personal interview, January 2, 2012.

(91) Buckle, 295.

(92) Mason, 207.

(93) Balanchine, George, and Francis Mason. *Balanchine's Complete Stories of the Great Ballets.* Revised and enlarged edition. Garden City, NY: Doubleday, 1977. 665.

(94) Balanchine and Mason, 666.

(95) Farrell, 213.

(96) Frank Ohman, personal interview, October 29, 2011.

(97) Taper 1984, 354.

(98) Daniel Duell, personal interview, December 29, 2011.

(99) Mason, 491.

(100) Taper 1984, 359–360.

(101) Buckle, 300.

(102) Mason, 592.

(103) Maynard, Olga. *The American Ballet.* Philadelphia: Macrae Smith, 1959. 78.

(104) de Mille, 183.

(105) Mason, 580.

(106) Buckle, 305.

(107) Frank Ohman, personal interview, October 29, 2011.

(108) Daniel Duell, personal interview, May 15, 2011.

(109) Farrell, 255.

(110) Mason, 501.

(111) Kisselgoff, Anna. "City Ballet: 'Pathetique' with Balanchine 'Adagio.'" *New York Times*, June 16, 1981. Web. Accessed August 29, 2010, at http://www.nytimes.com/1981/06/16/arts/city-ballet-pathetique-with-balanchine-adagio.html?&pagewanted=1.

(112) Anderson, Jack. "Lamentoso: Balanchine's Women with Their Hair Down." *New York Times*, July 19, 1981. Web. Accessed August 30, 2010 at http://www.nytimes.com/1981/07/09/arts/critic-s-notebook-lamentoso-balanchine-s-women-with-their-hair-down.html?&pagewanted=all.

(113) Mason, 597–598.

(114) Mason, 587.

(115) Daniel Duell, personal interview, December 29, 2011.

(116) Taper, 394.

(117) Buckle, 325.

(118) Mason, 575.

(119) Mason, 567.

(120) Daniel Duell, personal interview, January 4, 2012.

(121) Mason, 418.

(122) Taper 1984, 314.

Source List

"1968." Timeline description of the major political events in America in that year. Accessed on August 20, 2010, at http://www.nyu.edu/library/bobst/collections/exhibits/arch/1968/Index.html.

"Adelphi Theatre (New York)." *Wikipedia, the Free Encyclopedia.* Accessed on July 5, 2010, and April 28, 2011, at http://en.wikipedia.org/wiki/Adelphi_Theatre_(New_York).

"The Age of Anxiety." Article describes W. H. Auden's eclogue of that title and mentions that it inspired Leonard Bernstein's *Symphony No. 2 for Piano and Orchestra* and also Jerome Robbins' 1950 ballet *Age of Anxiety.* Accessed August 3, 2010, at http://en.wikipedia.org/wiki/The_Age_of_Anxiety.

Anderson, Jack. "The One and Only: The Ballet Russe de Monte Carlo. The Balanchine Years." *Ballet Review* 8, no. 4 (1980): 311–52.

Anderson, Jack. "Lamentoso: Balanchine's Women with Their Hair Down." *New York Times*, July 19, 1981, n.p. Accessed on August 30, 2010, at http://www.nytimes.com/1981/07/09/arts/criticsnotebook-lamentoso-balanchine-s-women-with-their-hair-down.html?&pagewanted=all.

Anderson, Zoë. "Balanchine's Don Quixote, Edinburgh Playhouse, Edinburgh." *The Independent* (online paper). Accessed August 20, 2010, from http://webcache.google-usercontent.com/search?q=cache:maAzcVd0TT4J:www.independent.co.uk/arts-entertainment/theatre-dance/reviews/balanchines-don-quixote-edinburgh-playhouse-edinburgh--none-onestar-threestar-fourstar-fivestar-

413957.html+review+of+Balanchine's+Don+Quixote&cd=1&hl= en&ct=clnk&gl=us.

Andros, Gus. "The Beginnings of Russian Ballet." *Michael Minn.* Accessed on January 5, 2010, at http://michaelminn.net/andros/index.php?beginnings_of_russian_ ballet, ©1997–2009.

Balanchine, George, and Francis Mason. *Balanchine's Complete Stories of the Great Ballets.* Revised and enlarged edi- tion. Garden City, NY: Doubleday, 1977.

"Ballet's Unfading Glory." (2005, March 5). *Kommersant, Russia's Daily Online.* Accessed on August 27, 2008, at http://74.125.95.104/search?q=cache:ilrogzKTdnkJ:www.komme rsant.com/p548973/r_1/Ballet_s_Unfading_Glory/+Maryinsky+t heatre+%2B+Lunacharsky&hl=en&ct=clnk&cd=8&gl=us.

Barnes, Clive. "The Dance: George Balanchine and the City Ballet. Two Programs Show a Master's Range." *New York Times*, December 1, 1966. Web.

Brinson, Peter, and Crisp, Clement. *The International Book of Ballet.* New York: Setin and Day, 1971.

Buckle, Richard. *George Balanchine: Ballet Master.* With John Taras. New York: Random House, 1988.

Coleman, Emily. "Apostle of the Pure Ballet." *New York Times,* December 1, 1957, pages 36, 38, 41, 48.

"Cuban Missile Crisis: Timeline." *Thinkquest.org.* Time- line of the U.S. discovery of Soviet missiles in Cuba aimed at the United States through their removal at Khrushchev's orders. Ac- cessed August 13, 2010, at http://library.thinkquest.org/11- 046/days/timeline.html.

D'Amboise, Jacques. *I Was a Dancer*. New York: Knopf, 2011.

Danilova, Alexandra. *Choura: The Memoirs of Alexandra Danilova*. New York: Knopf, 1986.

de Mille, Agnes. *The Book of the Dance*. New York: Golden Press, 1963.

Duberman, Martin. *The Worlds of Lincoln Kirstein*. New York: Knopf, 2007.

Farrell, Suzanne. *Holding On to the Air: An Autobiography*. With Toni Bentley. New York: Summit Books, 1990.

Fisher, Barbara Milberg. *In Balanchine's Company: A Dancer's Memoir*. Middletown, CT: Wesleyan University Press, 2006.

Fitzlyon, Kyril, and Tatiana Browning. *Before the Revolution: A View of Russia under the Last Tsar*. Woodstock, NY: Overlook Press, 1978.

Goldberg, Albert, in the *Los Angeles Times*, 9 June 1957, quoted in *West Pointe: The Ballet West Blog*. Accessed August 12, 2010, at http://www.balletwest.org/blog/page/14/.

Gottlieb, Robert. "Live Music Returns to City Ballet." *New York Observer,* December 12, 1999. Accessed August 27, 2010, at http://www.observer.com/1999/live-music-returns-city-ballet-theres-no-pulling-strings-polichenelles.

Gottlieb, Robert. *George Balanchine: The Ballet Maker*. New York: HarperCollins, 2004.

Greskovich, Robert. *Ballet 101: A Complete Guide to Learning and Loving the Ballet.* New York: Hyperion, 1998.

Gruen, John. *The Private World of Ballet.* New York: Viking Press, 1975.

Haggin, B. H. *Discovering Balanchine.* New York: Horizon Press, 1981.

"History." SPAC 2010. Saratoga Performing Arts Center. Accessed August 20, 2010, at http://spac.org/history.cfm.

Hurford, Daphne. *The Right Moves: A Dancer's Training.* New York: Atlantic Monthly Press, 1987.

"Jerome Robbins." Biography. *Wikipedia.org.* Accessed August 3, 2010, at http://en.wikipedia.org/wiki/Je-rome_Robbins.

Jordan, Stephanie. "Agon: A Musical/Choreographic Analysis." *Dance Research Journal* 25, no. 2 (1993): 1–12. Web. Accessed August 29, 2010, http://www.jstor.org/sta-ble/1478549.

Kisselgoff, Anna. "Balanchine's 'Mozartiana.'" *New York Times,* November 23, 1981. Accessed August 29, 2010, at http://www.nytimes.com/1981/11/23/arts/ci-ty-ballet-balanchine-s-mozartiana.html.

Kisselgoff, Anna. "City Ballet: 'Pathetique' with Balanchine 'Adagio.'" *New York Times,* June 16, 1981. Accessed August 29, 2010, at http://www.nytimes.com/19-81/06/16/arts/city-ballet-pathetique-with-balanchine-adagio.html?&pagewanted=1.

Kristy, Davida. *George Balanchine: American Ballet Master.* Minneapolis: Lerner, 1996.

"Leonide Massine Pt1." *Youtube.com.* Accessed July 20, 2010, at http://www.youtube.com/watch?v=0Hh_Trtv-zg.

"Leon Trotsky—Leader of the Red Army." *YouTube.com.* Accessed April 26, 2011, at http://www.you-tube.com/watch?v=u OHDfAfJB7.

Levin, Anne. "A Balanchine Blockbuster: How George Balanchine made *The Nutcracker* a Holiday Tradition." *Playbil-lArts.* Features: Dance. December 14, 2010. *PlaybillArts.com.* Accessed May 10, 2012, at http://www.play-billarts.com/features/article/8490.html.

"Mariinski Ballet." *Wikipedia.org.* Accessed May 6, 2011, at http://en.wikipedia.org/wiki/Mariinsky_Ballet.

Markova, Dame Alicia. *Markova Remembers.* London: H. Hamilton, 1986.

Martin, John. "Stravinsky Work in World Premiere: Ballet Society Features His *Orpheus* at City Center to Balanchine Dance." *New York Times,* April 29, 1948.

Martin, John. "Dance III: New York City Ballet in Final Section of Tenth Anniversary Celebration." *New York Times,* May 10, 1959.

Martins, Peter. *Far from Denmark.* Boston: Little, Brown, 1982.

Mason, Francis. *I Remember Balanchine: Recollections of the Ballet Master by Those Who Knew Him.* New York: Double-day, 1991.

Maynard, Olga. *The American Ballet.* Philadelphia, PA: Macrae Smith, 1959.

"Nicholas Magallanes." *Wikipedia.org.* Accessed July 30, 2010, at http://en.wikipedia.org/wiki/Ni-cholas_Magallanes.

Pipes, Richard. *Russia under the Bolshevik Regime.* New York: Knopf, 1993.

Reiter, Susan. "Hugo Fiorato." *Playbill*, May 1, 2004.

Rockwell, John. "Balanchine's 'Don Quixote,' Revived by His Dulcinea." *New York Times*, June 24, 2005. Accessed August 20, 2010, at http://www.nytimes.com/2005/06/24/arts/dance/24farr.html.

Smith, Sid. "Ballet Chicago's Balanchine Full of Thrills." *Chicago Tribune,* May 15, 2011. Accessed May 16, 2011, and May 6, 2012, at http://articles.chicagotribune.com/2011-05-15/entertainment/ct-live-0516-balanchine-celebration-20110515_1_ted-seymour-rachel-jambois-george-balanchine-trust.

"Soviet Union: The Soviet Family." *Library of Congress Country Studies,* found under *LOC.gov.* Accessed May 4, 2012, http://rs6.loc.gov/cgi-bin/query/r?frd/cstdy:@field(DOCID+su0162).

"Stravinsky: The Flood." Stravinsky's piece with notes from the posting entity, NewMusicXX. *YouTube.com.* Accessed July 20, 2010, and also June 29, 2012, at http://www.youtube.com/watch?v=Ogzi7QGy63g.

Stuart, Otis. "On Her Own." *New York City Ballet News*, Fall 1986 (3-86), p. 10.

Sundram, Jason. *Program Notes: Symphony No. 6 in B minor Pathetique Opus 74 (1893).* Accessed August 30, 2010, at

http://webcache.googleusercontent.com/search?q=cache:zxPGA
mquK6YJ:jsundram.freeshell.org/ProgramNotes/Tchaikovsky_S
ympho-
ny.html+Russian+orthodox+requiem+in+Pathetique&cd=4&hl=e
n&ct=clnk&gl=us.

Taper, Bernard, *Balanchine: A Biography.* New York:
Harper & Row, 1963.

Taper, Bernard. *Balanchine: A Biography.* New York:
Times Books, 1984.

Teachout, Terry. *All in the Dances: A Brief Life of George
Balanchine.* Orlando, FL: Harcourt, 2004.

"Television History—The First 75 Years." *TVhistory.TV.*
Accessed July 17, 2011, http://www.tvhistory.tv/1946-1949.htm.

Tracy, Robert, with Sharon DeLano. *Balanchine's Ballerinas: Conversations with the Muses.* New York: Linden
Press/Simon & Schuster, 1983.

Vaill, Amanda. *Somewhere: The Life of Jerome Robbins.*
New York: Broadway Books, 2006.

"Vienna Waltzes." Web page describing Balanchine's ballet as listed in the New York City Ballet's Repertory Index. Accessed August 27, 2010, at http://www.nycballet.com/com-
pany/rep.html?rep=212.

Villella, Edward. *Prodigal Son: Dancing for Balanchine in
a World of Pain and Magic.* With Larry Kaplan. New York: Simon and Schuster, 1992.

Zorina, Vera. *Zorina.* New York: Farrar Strauss Giroux,
1986.

Index

Made in the USA
Charleston, SC
16 October 2012